The Path

THE PATH

HOW TO JOURNEY WITH GOD AND LIVE YOUR PURPOSE

SCHLYCE JIMENEZ

NEW YORK

LONDON • NASHVILLE • MELBOURNE • VANCOUVER

The Path

How to Journey with God and Live Your Purpose

Published in New York, New York, by Morgan James Publishing in partnership with Difference Press. Morgan James is a trademark of Morgan James, LLC.
www.MorganJamesPublishing.com

ISBN 9781642792027 paperback
ISBN 9781642792034 eBook
Library of Congress Control Number: 2018952109

Cover Design by:
Megan Dillon
megan@creativeninjadesigns.com

Interior Design by:
Chris Treccani
www.3dogcreative.net

Morgan James is a proud partner of Habitat for Humanity Peninsula and Greater Williamsburg. Partners in building since 2006.

Get involved today! Visit
MorganJamesPublishing.com/giving-back

For my precious mother, who first introduced me to Jesus and recognized the call of God on my life at a young age. Thank you for praying for me, believing in me, and seeing me through the eyes of Love especially in the "dark years," when I rejected the faith, thinking religion and Jesus were one and the same. Mom, you are greatly loved and missed every day. Your prayers continue to be answered in my life.

TABLE OF CONTENTS

The Father has given me all these things to do and say. This is a unique Father-Son operation, coming out of Father and Son intimacies and knowledge. No one knows the Son the way the Father does, nor the Father the way the Son does. But I'm not keeping it to myself; I'm ready to go over it line by line with anyone willing to listen.

– Jesus

INTRODUCTION

The meaning of life is to find your gift. The purpose of life is to give it away.
– Pablo Picasso

What is the reason for my existence? What is the meaning of my life? Is there a purpose for the universe, creation, and man? These questions lurk deep within the hearts of everyone regardless of race, ethnic heritage, socioeconomic status, or nationality. Throughout human history, various philosophers and religions have attempted to answer these questions. Why? Because the deepest craving of the human spirit is to find purpose, meaning, and significance in life. Consciously or unconsciously, admitted or unadmitted, directly or indirectly, the internal passion for relevance and self-expression is what motivates and drives human beings.

I wrote this book to help you discover your very own God-breathed answers to the most significant questions you will ever ask and answer.

Who is God?
Who am I?
Why am I here?
Where am I headed?
How do I get there?

You were born for a reason. You are God's dream – a manifestation of the desires of His heart. And in case you forgot, God is a big dreamer. If you ever doubt that, Google the size of the universe just for grins. As God's dream, your dreams are also His dreams. Your story is part of His story. Maybe you've never thought about it quite like this before. If not, you are in for a huge surprise. God is better than you've imagined Him to be.

Your Dreams Glorify God

Here is a newsflash a lot of people have never read – God wants you to live the life of your dreams. Yes, you heard me correctly. God is not the suffer-to-teach-you-a-lesson God you may have been warned about by your well-meaning Sunday school teacher. The truth is way more exciting. When you live the life of your dreams, God is glorified. Your dreams reveal His true nature. They prove just how good of a Dad He really is. In actuality, it is religion, as in the *spirit of religion* – you know, the one that drove the Pharisees to crucify Jesus – that hates dreams and, for that matter, dreamers. According to religion, serving God is supposed to be miserable, a sack-cloth-and-ashes kind of miserable, with a focus on self-depreciation, lifeless spiritual disciplines, and vigilant resistance of temptations. Hogwash, friends! Hogwash! God wants you to enjoy your life. It's the reason Jesus was born. The purpose of Jesus' life was for you to enjoy yours.

> *I came that they may have and enjoy life, and have it in abundance*
> *[to the full, till it overflows].*
> – John 10:10 (AMP)

Purpose Gives Life Meaning

Deciding to pursue a life of purpose is one of the most important and fulfilling choices you can make in life. Sadly, very few people take the leap. Most people alive on the planet today are not clear about their life purpose. Of the almost 7.5 billion people in the world today, only a very small percentage, around 5% or less, can describe their life purpose with crystal-clear clarity. An even smaller percentage, less than 2%, are living a life that authentically expresses their purpose. The majority of people are not living the life of their dreams. The norm, unfortunately, is purposeless living.

If that sounds incredible to you, I agree. It seems almost impossible that 98% of the people alive on the planet today are not living the life of their dreams. But, if you think about it, in your circle of friends, family, coworkers, neighbors, etc., how many would you say can articulate their life purpose or consider themselves living a purposeful life? For most people, these statistics prove true. Honestly, nothing makes me sadder. The idea that the majority of people live their entire lives without ever knowing the reason for their existence is beyond tragic. Having a sense of purpose is what gives meaning to our lives. Pursuing our dreams is what makes life exciting and worthwhile. Having a vision for our lives is what gives us a sense of direction.

Purposeless Living Is Painful

The consequences of purposeless living are evident all around us. Depression, hopelessness, addiction, and even suicide are the sad reality for many people living day after day without having a concrete reason to do so. For others, their days are overshadowed by an underlying sense of dissatisfaction. It is not that life is horrible, necessarily, it is just unfulfilling. They wake up every day, dreading their day. Maybe they feel stuck in the wrong relationship, a dead-end job, or both. For others, they feel bored stiff with their lives. They've lost a sense of wonder and adventure. When you don't know the reason for your existence, life can feel monotonous and mundane, like you are running on a treadmill to nowhere, just going through the motions of living.

A lot of people who have yet to discover their purpose intuitively know something is missing and they need to make changes, but for reasons they can't really identify, they don't. Most cannot put their finger on what is missing. This is why purposelessness can feel so frustrating and hopeless. The majority of people can't figure out exactly what their problem actually is. When they evaluate their lives, there are things they like, dislike, and want to change, but they can also look around on any given day, compare themselves to others who are worse off than they are, and choose to count their blessings.

There Has to Be More

Feeling bad about your life, for a lot of people, feels wrong. Especially when you consider all of the people who might not know where their next meal is coming from or who are living in the middle of a war zone. More likely than not, there are a lot of people in the world who have it much worse than you. So, a lot of people never give themselves permission to really get to the bottom of what is actually missing in their lives. They feel guilty about feeling dissatisfied with their lives because they figure it's *not that bad.*

There are others who choose, consciously or subconsciously, to never take the time to think about any of it. Instead, they keep themselves busy with all kinds of activities – work, family, entertainment, social engagements – you name it. They never take the time to stop and think about what really matters in life. But, truthfully, no matter how hard people try to avoid it, on some level, when you don't know your purpose, you can never shake the nagging feeling that something is missing in your life. When things finally settle down after yet another long and busy day, subtle thoughts invariably creep in, "There has to be more."

Somewhere between the dreams of your childhood and the responsibility of being a grown-up, the daily grind of life tends to hijack your destiny. When this happens, it is normal to feel lost and conflicted inside. The child in you still wants life to be fun. The dreamer in you is still dreaming. Yet, the adult in you is telling everyone to get to work, pay the bills, and be responsible. This, of course, is why so many people live for weekends and dread Mondays. Weekends feel like their "real life" and everything else feels like the price they have to pay to live it. Nicknames like "Weekend Warrior" and the 80s anthem "Working for the Weekend" pay homage to this dismal reality.

What's most unfortunate about all of this, though, is how time keeps on ticking. Day after day, month after month, year after year, the sand in the hourglass keeps falling. Then, before you know it, you have reached the end of your life having never really lived it. Sometimes, especially during times of personal tragedy such as the loss of a loved one, you are reminded how short life really is. You might even stop to ponder the idea that there's more to life than what you are experiencing. But usually for the most part, these moments of clarity are short-lived. The routines of life have a tendency to rock you back to sleep pretty quickly. As a result, the dreams in your heart stay buried and the longing to live a life of significance remains unfulfilled.

If there is a bright side to the purposeless epidemic, it feels like a personal one. Because so many people are struggling to live lives that matter, every day I get the awesome opportunity of helping people from all walks of life find the path to purpose. As a result, they are living the life of their dreams, making a difference, and finding fulfillment and meaning in their lives. I love what I do. It is incredibly fulfilling to make a difference helping other people make a difference.

Your Potential Is Unfathomable

If there's one thing I've learned after spending countless hours with people on the path to purpose, it is this: Human beings are magnificent creations. We are created in God's image, and our potential is unimaginable. The seemingly impossible dreams in our hearts are evidence of this. No matter how impossible it may seem, if you can dream it, you can be it. Human history, as dramatic, tragic, and triumphant as it has been, is filled with stories of people whose dreams literally changed the world. Driven by a dream, people have overcome seemingly incredible odds to serve humanity, vanquish evil, and make a difference. Nelson Mandela, Joan of Arc, Mozart, Helen Keller, Henry Ford, Rosa Parks, Sir Isaac Newton, Lady Diana, and Martin Luther King are just a few examples of people who left an indelible mark on our world. In scripture, people such as Moses, King David, Queen Esther, the Apostle Paul, and, of course, Jesus fulfilled their life purpose and are still influencing the world today.

Sometimes, it's easy to think of ourselves in a completely different category from famous world changers and to think, "Who am I to change the world?" But if everyone thought that way, we would still be living in the Dark Ages. Every single world changer I just listed, including Jesus, was at some point just a regular person. Jesus started out as a carpenter, for goodness sake! But that is the beauty of purpose. It is an equal-opportunity employer. Everyone on the planet was born with one. And everyone has an equal opportunity to discover it.

Ultimately, at the end of the day, it's not the number of people you impact; it's the cumulative effect of your life. In Jesus' life, for example, He spent the majority of His time with just 12 people, His disciples. He taught several thousand people on occasion and healed multitudes, but really, He changed the world through the lives of just a few individuals. There were only 120 people in the upper room on the day of Pentecost. Yet, those 120 people turned the world upside down. That's why it isn't just how big of a difference you personally make in your lifetime that matters. God's plans are always much bigger than one person's life. What you were born to accomplish in this life fits perfectly into God's overall big picture for the planet. Your only goal is to discover and fulfill *your* divine purpose. No one but God knows the cumulative effect and the impact of your life. But it's very possible that your life purpose has the potential to change cities, nations, and the world.

Now Is Your Time

God has created every person on the planet for a purpose. If you've yet to discover yours, let me assure you it's not too late. The purpose train didn't leave the station without you. I love the way the scripture found in Ecclesiastes 3:1 explains it:

> *To everything there is a season, a time for every purpose under heaven.*
> – Ecclesiastes 3:1 (KJV)

You haven't missed your opportunity to live your purpose. As this scripture indicates, there is a time for your purpose. There is a time for you to discover it. There is a time for you to pursue it. And there is a time for it to be fulfilled. No matter how young or old you are, *right now* is the perfect time for your purpose. Consider this book a divine appointment with your future destiny. Trust the timing is just right for you to discover your life purpose. Treat it as a sign from heaven. The cry of your heart that longs to live a life of significance is being answered.

If that seems a bit crazy to you, here's what your head needs to hear about your heart. Your need for significance and fulfillment is valid. Maybe you remember studying Abraham Maslow's hierarchy of needs in high school. In Maslow's needs hierarchy, once your basic needs for food, water, shelter, and safety are met, your higher psychological needs begin to kick in. The need for love, a sense of belonging, and esteem begin to guide you toward the things that will fulfill these needs. Once these needs are met, you turn your attention to your highest need, the need to develop your full potential and experience self-actualization. Maslow discovered what scripture had already revealed. Human beings are hard-wired with the need to have a purpose and vision for their lives and develop their full potential.

Where there is no vision, the people perish.
– Proverbs 29:18a (KJV)

Ever heard the old saying, "When the student is ready the teacher appears?" I would like you to consider that you are not reading this book by accident. What if the deepest unmet needs of your heart, like a compass, directed you to this book? What if it's a divine wake-up call? What if you are now standing in the sacred place where the noise of your life can no longer drown out your call to greatness? The Psalmist David describes this place as "deep calling unto deep," where the silent cry of your heart is answered by the cry of God's heart.

You, my friend, are ready. This is your time. Together, we are about to embark on the adventure of a lifetime to discover what's been missing from your life, your true life purpose. You are about to dive deep, into the depths of God's heart, to find answers to some of the most important questions a human being can ask and answer. In the process, you will be lifted off the beaten path that everyone seems to be blindly following and onto your very own path – the one that leads to your divine destiny and true fulfillment and meaning in life.

CHAPTER ONE

Sleepwalking through Life

Life is either a daring adventure, or nothing.
– Helen Keller

No matter how successful you may appear to be, without knowing your life purpose, you will always feel like something is missing from your life. You aren't crazy. You're perfectly sane. Something very important *is* missing from your life – the *reason* for your life. So don't beat yourself up for feeling the way you do. Don't try to talk yourself out of it or ignore your feelings. Instead, lean into the discomfort and embrace your heart. Life is way too short to sleepwalk through it, unaware of what you're missing.

If you've ever seen the movie *The Truman Show,* you know that everything in Truman Burbank's (Jim Carrey's) life, even though he doesn't know it, is part of a massive TV set. His life isn't what it seems. Like living in the Twilight Zone, something is wrong; something is unreal about the world he knows. Part of what makes *The Truman Show* so intriguing is that, on some level, we all feel this way, at least sometimes. There has to be more to life, and more to you, than what you've experienced thus far. It's hard to describe the feeling, but something just feels *off*. The sensation takes many forms. Maybe it's a discomforting sense of futility that keeps you up at night. Or maybe is an unshakable feeling that the years are flying by with little or no progress. Or maybe it sounds like your internal critic that is always berating you and beating you up over where you are in life. It may be hard to describe. But deep down you feel disappointed that you are not all you want to be and know you should be. You are haunted by the dreams you never pursued. Secretly, you struggle with a gnawing sensation that creeps into your consciousness now and then: Is this all there is? For some odd reason, you thought there'd be more.

You Aren't Crazy or Alone

Connecting with the gnawing sense of dissatisfaction you feel, as unpleasant as it may be, is a necessary first step toward waking up to the life you were born to live. It's okay that you're unhappy living a normal life. It's perfectly fine that you're not satisfied with the status quo. Maybe you weren't created to be normal. Maybe you were never designed for the ordinary. Maybe, just maybe, you were born to do something significant.

Every day, I get the privilege of working with big dreamers, people who refuse to live normal lives. It's extremely rewarding to be surrounded by people who are going for it. You see, helping people find the path to their divine purpose is my divine purpose. My big dream is helping big dreamers fulfill their dreams. But, like most of my clients and students, I wasn't always so clear. I didn't know the things I'm sharing with you in this book. I actually thought there was something wrong with me for feeling so dissatisfied with my life. I didn't know that most of the time, waking up to your divine purpose and answering the call to greatness requires that you reach the point in your life where you can't stand your life any longer. But, think about it. It makes sense. You don't try to diagnose a problem you don't think you have.

Take Jenna, for example. She's a graduate of Emerge School of Transformation, my program that helps people hear from God about their true life purpose and develop a real relationship with Him. When Jenna started the program, she was feeling stuck in a life that felt monotonous and unfulfilling. She had yet to discover her divine purpose. She was a successful executive in a growing organization, but her job didn't feel like her calling. She kept experiencing this persistent feeling that the things she'd gone through in life could help other people.

She had what she would have called a decent relationship with God, but she also feared that if she asked Him about her life purpose, it might be something she didn't want to actually do. She hadn't yet made the connection – God is The Ultimate Dream Giver. The dreams He plants in our hearts always fulfill our deepest desires. Thankfully, as Jenna went through Emerge and got to know God for who He really is, she released her fears and overcame her wrong image of God as someone who delights in suffering. As a result, her heart was set free to dream big and discover God's purpose for her life.

Today, after graduating from the program, Jenna is a published author and successful mentor to single women from all over the globe. She is helping people celebrate their singleness and become powerful women who aren't defined by their romantic relationships. She's making a huge difference in people's lives because she heard from God about her divine purpose. She wakes up every day excited to communicate with God about how to fulfill her dream of becoming a person of influence who makes a difference in the world. She's an inspiration to a whole lot of people, including me.

There's Only One You

Of the billions and billions of people on the planet, there is only one of you. Let that sink in for a minute. Just like your fingerprints, you are one of a kind. That's why you shouldn't allow anyone to make you feel inferior or average. This is also one of the reasons it's so important to listen to your own heart. If you aren't following your heart, who or what are you following? You can search outside of yourself until you are blue in the face, going to conferences, reading books, and listening to all kinds of wonderful wisdom, but in the end, God placed your purpose inside of you. He planted eternity in your heart.

> *Yet God has made everything beautiful for its own time. He has planted eternity in the human heart, but even so, people cannot see the whole scope of God's work from beginning to end.*
> – Ecclesiastes 3:11 (NLT)

The dreams in your heart matter. They are proof that your life is intended by God to have significance and meaning. They are God's clues to help you discover your divine purpose. You were not born to wander aimlessly through life, following the crowd. God intended for you to follow your heart like a compass and blaze your own trail. Until you do, you'll always feel like something is missing.

The poorest person in the world isn't someone without the basic necessities of life. It's the person living without purpose. Living a life you aren't passionate about is no way to live at all. It's actually a subtle form of torture. Life isn't supposed to feel like an endless string of activities that leave you feeling drained at the end of every day. You weren't designed by God to live a mediocre, mundane existence. You were born to make a difference, to bless others with your unique gifts, talents, and life experiences. Whether you realize it or not, you are an answer to someone's prayer.

God has an incredible purpose, plan, and vision for every person on the planet, including you. And He wants you to discover it more than you do. You are His idea. You are His dream. Your becoming all that He created you to be not only satisfies the deepest longing of your heart, it also satisfies the deepest longings of God's heart. Jesus paid an incredible price, *His own life*, so that you could live yours to the fullest.

> *I came so that they could have life —*
> *indeed, so that they could live life to the fullest.*
> – John 10:10 (CEB)

But you'll never find what you're looking for by searching for it outside of yourself. This is why it's so important to revere your individuality, honor your spirit, and listen to your heart. Your deepest desires are Divine. As you give them an audience, you'll be amazed at what they will tell you about yourself, God, and your life purpose. Don't let time keep "slippin', slippin', slippin' into the future." Set your heart free. Give yourself permission to fly.

It's Never Too Late

No matter how old you are, it's never too late to ask yourself what you want to be when you grow up. What does age have to do with living a life of purpose? Whether you are 16 or 69, age is only a limitation if you allow it to be. There are plenty of people on the planet who are making a difference in their teens. There are also lots of people who are making a difference later in life. Right up until you take your last breath, you have the opportunity to live a life of purpose.

Take Dr. Randy Pausch, a college professor who taught at Carnegie Mellon, for example. His last lecture before dying of pancreatic cancer inspired people from all over the world to recognize the brevity of life and live life with child-like wonder. As the video of his lecture went viral across the globe, it was translated into many languages and became the basis of a best-selling book. Time magazine named Dr. Pausch one of the 100 most influential people in the world, and ABC declared him one of its three "persons of the year" for 2007. He even appeared on Oprah Winfrey's television show before his death, to give a condensed version of his lecture.

Even on your deathbed, you can live a life of significance and purpose. But you don't have to wait until you're dying to find a reason to live. Maybe you used to know what you wanted to do with your life, but life circumstances seemed to take you another direction. You gave up your dream of becoming a famous artist to start a family or at one time you wanted to start your own business and give millions away to charity, but you never felt the time was right. There are always reasons, usually very valid ones, to keep putting your dreams on hold. But, thankfully, there's no expiration date on dreams. You can discover your life purpose anytime you decide to find it. You can answer the call to greatness at any age.

The call to greatness sounds different at different times in our lives. You may first hear it as a quiet, but persistent, thought – "What's wrong with my life. Something is missing." As time passes, it may grow more intense, like an unquenchable thirst. You can't escape the idea that there's absolutely something you must do in your lifetime. At other times, it's simply the dream that won't go away. There is something you've always dreamed about doing that seems to consistently get put on the back burner. However it comes, stop letting the call to greatness go to voicemail. Recognize it for what it is and listen to your heart. Asking yourself what you want your life to be about, while you still have life to live, is vital. Fulfilling your purpose is the only thing that gives your life true meaning. It makes life make sense.

The Missing Link

Don't be like the majority of people, who discount their dreams and the subtle cry of their heart to make a difference in the world. If the work you are doing isn't something you seriously care about, then it's not your purpose in life to be doing it. It is time to begin to ask yourself some serious why questions like "Why am I living my life like this is all there is?" Your dreams aren't selfish; they are important. You are alive in this moment for a reason. The world is filled with amazing people, with incredible gifts and unbelievable potential, who are expending their time and energy on things that, in the end, won't amount to a hill of beans or matter much in the grand scheme of things. The real tragedy of most people's lives, no matter how much they endured in life, is that they'll go to their graves never having experienced the joy of living a purpose-filled life.

The journey to finding your purpose and living a life of your dreams may not be the easiest path. But it's the only one worth taking. Yes, you have to confront your deepest fears and ask yourself some really hard questions. But you aren't alone on your journey and the answers you seek can be found. Ultimately, the quest for purpose is a spiritual one. It requires that you get to know the One who created you and who knows everything about you. Besides, He's been waiting to talk to you about your purpose for a really long time – since the beginning of time, actually.

For we are His workmanship [His own master work, a work of art], created in Christ Jesus [reborn from above – spiritually transformed, renewed, ready to be used] for good works, which God prepared [for us] beforehand [taking paths which He set], so that we would walk in them [living the good life which He prearranged and made ready for us].
– Ephesians 2:10 (AMP)

Since God is the author of your purpose, it goes without saying that you need to talk to Him about it. But talking to God – and hearing from Him with the same clarity you would with anyone else – isn't something most people know how to do. It can feel like an overwhelming undertaking. Plus, there are a lot of people in the world who think you are crazy for even having the expectation of talking to God. Heck, I used to think that way. When I was in my twenties, if you told me you were having conversations with God, I would have thought you needed to get measured for a straightjacket. But, thankfully, I've come a long way since then. Talking with God is actually a lot easier than you think. I've personally taught thousands of people how to hear God's voice and use their spiritual senses to interact with Him. I've taught children, teenagers, and adults of all ages how to hear God with confidence. There's not a single one of my clients or students who aren't proficient at it. There's not a single Emerger (someone enrolled in the Emerge School of Transformation) who isn't hearing their own God-breathed answers to the questions most people never seem to know how to answer. They are hearing God as clearly as they do their own thoughts.

Ready to Go for It?

Sound impossible? Well, buckle your seatbelt. Our journey together over the course of you reading this book is going to change your perspective on what's impossible. I'll be sharing the very same principles that my clients and students are learning every day. You can hear God about your divine purpose. In fact, you can experience the same level of intimacy with God that Jesus enjoyed with the Father. I know that may sound crazy, but one of my favorite scriptures in the entire Bible promises this to anyone who is willing to go for it. You don't have to be super-intelligent or a religious scholar to hear God. You just have to be willing to listen.

> *Abruptly Jesus broke into prayer: "Thank you, Father, Lord of heaven and earth. You've concealed your ways from sophisticates and know-it-alls, but spelled them out clearly to ordinary people. Yes, Father, that's the way you like to work." Jesus resumed talking to the people, but now tenderly. "The Father has given me all these things to do and say. This is a unique Father-Son operation, coming out of Father and Son intimacies and knowledge. No one knows the Son the way the Father does, nor the Father the way the Son does. But I'm not keeping it to myself; I'm ready to go over it line by line with anyone willing to listen."*
> Matthew 11:25–27 (MSG)

I want you to take a moment to really let that scripture sink in. This is such an incredible promise. Read the verse again and maybe get out a highlighter and underline the part that says how Jesus is ready to go over how to know the Father the way He does, *line by line*. If you are like me, this scripture both fascinates and challenges. I'm fascinated that Jesus Himself is willing to help us develop the same kind of intimate relationship He has with the Father. I'm also challenged to not let myself, or for that matter anyone else that I work with, settle for less. This scripture really hits it home and explains why I do what I do. Yes, it thrills me to help people find their purpose. But the ultimate thrill comes from *how* they find their purpose. Helping people get to know the Father, like Jesus knew the Father, so that they can discover their life purpose is what makes my job so rewarding.

As I wrap up this chapter, I want to leave you with a note from the Father that I believe will really encourage you. I often write these little love notes – I call them Kisses from Heaven – to the people who are a part of my tribe. I'll send them via email or post them on social media every so often. I wanted to incorporate one at the end of every chapter so that you're hearing not only from me in this book but also from the One who I believe led you to read the book in the first place.

Let me give you a little more insight about inspired messages from God. Each of the love notes from Dad I've included in this book is a *prophecy*. Don't be intimidated by the term. *Prophecy* is simply the scriptural term that describes a divinely inspired message or revelation given to someone or a group of people. The Bible says prophecy is a message given by someone who speaks from God as the Holy Spirit moves them (2 Peter 1:20–21). As they receive God's message, they speak it to others (Acts 3:18).

Prophecy is one of the nine gifts of the Spirit described in 1 Corinthians 12:8–10. All throughout the Bible, the Holy Spirit guided the thoughts of His messengers to convey His words. This is the sense of the Bible's statement: "All Scripture is inspired of God." The phrase "inspired of God" can also be rendered "God-breathed" (2 Timothy 3:16, TEB). God uses His Holy Spirit to "breathe" His ideas and words into the minds of His messenger. With prophecy, the message is God's, but the messenger selects the wording (2 Samuel 12:1–2).

There's obviously a ton more I could share with you about prophecy, the gifts of the Spirit, and how to receive divinely inspired messages from God. But, for now, suffice it to say, read the love note as it is intended – as a personal note from God your Father. Don't overthink it. Just receive it. The Holy Spirit's gifts are to be opened and enjoyed like every other gift you receive.

After the love note, you will find a Digging Deeper Exercise that I encourage you to take the time to work through. I've included Digging Deeper Exercises at the end of each chapter to help you develop your ability to experience God and hear from Him about your life purpose. In this chapter's Digging Deeper Exercise, you'll be creating what I call a "Journey Journal." As we embark on the journey to hearing from God about your life purpose, your Journey Journal will become one of the most important ways you practice hearing from God. Over time, it will become your go-to place for times of quiet reflection, contemplation, and seeking wisdom from God.

Your faithfulness to start and continue the journaling process, both while reading this book and afterward, will lead to greater inner peace, self-acceptance, and self-care. It will also lead you into deeper levels of worship and intimacy with God as you continue to invite God into your innermost thoughts and the most vulnerable places in your heart. It will help you take your relationship with God to a whole new level, and I promise you, you will never be the same. I cannot wait for you to get started. I am so excited to be on this journey with you.

Love Note from Dad

My Blessed Child,

 I cannot tell you how eager and excited I am to have you join Me on the path to discovering your purpose. I have so many extraordinary things to tell you and show you. The journey is going to be such a marvelous adventure. I am especially looking forward to you starting to see things from a whole new perspective. Seeing yourself as I see you is going to transform your life in ways you've never imagined. Recognizing how much I love you is going to bring such stability and peace into your life. Peering into your future and grasping all of the incredible things I have prepared for you is going to take your breath away. You are standing on the precipice of a whole new outlook on everything.

 You see, the path to purpose transforms everything. As we walk together, step by step along the path, you will see the illusions that have limited you for what they are — just illusions. As a result, impossible dreams, bigger than the ones you have dreamed thus far, will be within your reach. Because the truth of the matter is this: No one has ever seen or heard of anything quite like you before, beloved. You are my exquisite masterpiece. Created in My image and full of My glory. I've hidden Myself inside of you, My child, and My glory is your glory. Revealing who you are and the reason you were born is My delight. It's the unveiling of My masterpiece. It's the manifestation of My glory. So take My hand, child, and let's skip down the path together. Now is the time for you to see just how glorious I created you to be.

Kisses from Heaven,
Dad

Digging Deeper Exercise - Creating a Journey Journal

STEP 1 - Buy Yourself a New Journal

There is something about a new journal that always feels like a new beginning. So whether you've been journaling for years or you've never journaled a day in your life, invest in a brand new journal for yourself. The purpose of this journal is to create a sacred space for you to connect with God – to be authentic with yourself and with God and to document your experiences and process your innermost thoughts with God.

In addition, here's a few more benefits from journaling your journey to discover your life purpose:

- Journaling provides a quiet space where your sense of self is cultivated.
- Journaling helps you become more self-aware and honest with yourself and God.
- Journaling gives you a sacred space to process your thoughts, where you are strengthened and encouraged, and your relationship with God becomes more personal and real.
- Journaling creates a safe place – sometimes referred to as the secret place in scripture, or your prayer closet – where you can be alone with God.
- Journaling aids the reflective process, like looking into a mirror on paper; it helps you more objectively see yourself and your life.
- Journaling your conversations with God is one of the best ways to grow in your ability to hear from Him.

STEP 2 - Write Out Matthew 11:25-27

As a reminder of Jesus' awesome promise to help you develop the same kind of relationship He had with the Father, write out Matthew 11:25–27 from the Message Translation on the front page of your new journal. I encourage you to read the scripture often as a reminder of why you are keeping a Journey Journal and to help you release your faith to receive Jesus' promise.

Abruptly Jesus broke into prayer: "Thank you, Father, Lord of heaven and earth. You've concealed your ways from sophisticates and know-it-alls, but spelled them out clearly to ordinary people. Yes, Father, that's the way you like to work." Jesus resumed talking to the people, but now tenderly. "The Father has given me all these things to do and say. This is a unique Father-Son operation, coming out of Father and Son intimacies and knowledge. No one knows the Son the way the Father does, nor the Father the way the Son does. But I'm not keeping it to myself; I'm ready to go over it line by line with anyone willing to listen."
– Matthew 11:25–27 (MSG)

STEP 3 - Begin with a Letter to God

The very first entry in your new journal is going to be a letter to God letting Him know you'd like to develop a deeper relationship with Him, specifically the kind that Jesus enjoyed. If you've never written a letter to God before, don't worry. It's really easy. You just write it the way you would talk to anyone else. God's actually very approachable. He's nothing like the spirit of religion has portrayed Him to be. Just talk to Him as if He were hanging out in your living room with you or having coffee with you at Starbucks.

Don't worry about saying the right or wrong things. The point is just to be real. Remember, the whole purpose of writing a letter to Him is to get to know Him better. The letter is you simply sharing your desire to have a deeper relationship with Him. It's a tangible way for you to give Him permission to reveal Himself to you in greater dimensions and different ways from how you've previously experienced.

If there are things standing in the way of you getting real with God, such as problems you have with Him, guilt, or people you need to forgive, then just be real about those things. God knows about it anyway, so just tell Him how you feel. If you're angry or sad or feeling unworthy, then discuss it with Him. Let Him know that you are inviting Him into your innermost thoughts and emotions, trusting that since He knows about it already, there's really no reason to try to hide it anyway.

Also, take some time to be grateful in your letter. Write to God about things you are thankful for and ways that you know you are blessed. If there are specific things you'd like to "pray about," make sure to include those as well. But most importantly and above all, be real. Remember God is not just God; He's your Friend and Father. He's created you for fellowship because He loves you. He's known you before the worlds were ever created and specifically led you to this very moment – whether you realize it or not.

CHAPTER TWO

Hitting the Snooze Button

I always wanted to be somebody. I should have been more specific.
– Lily Tomlin

I was dying and I knew it. I just didn't know what to do about it. No, I wasn't physically dying. I was dying on the inside. I felt like a zombie who is *alive* in a sense, but also not really living. Trying to escape my feelings as the primary way of dealing with my problems had taken its toll. I felt like I was losing my mind and my therapist's diagnosis wasn't good. I was deeply depressed and my anxiety level was off the chart. To make matters worse, the coping mechanisms I had developed to deal with my out-of-control feelings were no longer working. I was single, without a romantic relationship to help me feel better about myself, for the first time since being a teenager. The hangovers, after a night out with friends, were lasting for days and making me feel even crazier. Spending money as fast as I could make it was stressing me out. Something had to change. I was at the end of the road that led to nowhere and I felt like I was out of options.

Looking back, I can see how my entire life had led me to this moment. Here, at 33 years old, I had become a professional "pain manager." At the time, I didn't know how to make the pain stop and I hadn't yet met the only One who could actually take the pain away. In many ways, my life was extremely successful.

I had just finished remodeling my beautiful high-rise condo that overlooked Lake Michigan in Chicago's Gold Coast. I was one of the top performers at the Fortune 500 software company where I worked. I had lots of friends and plenty of money to live the so-called high -life. But I was losing my grip. I had moved to Chicago to start my life over, but the change of geography didn't change who I was. I couldn't outrun myself.

It's a pretty sobering reality to come to the place where you feel like a walking dead person. Life loses its color. It feels like you're living in a black and white movie. You know there's more than what you are experiencing, but you can't see it. Something big is missing, but you haven't got a clue about what it might be. You feel hopeless, helpless, and empty inside and nothing you do seems to make it go away. There's an old saying often quoted by the likes of Tony Robbins and Dr. Henry Cloud that perfectly describes the place I had come to in my life.

> *People only change when the pain of staying the same*
> *outweighs the pain of change.*
> – Anonymous

Fortunately or unfortunately, depending on how you look at it, this is exactly the place I found myself. Something had to change. I simply could not live another day without really living. The pain had to stop. I had to discover the truth that would set me free.

Something Is Missing

Looking back on my life now, it's very clear to me how I ended up in this very dark place without a clue about the true meaning of life. It's also clear to me how in the end, it was all a divine setup that perfectly prepared me for my life purpose.

I can vividly remember myself as a kid thinking about the meaning of my life. I grew up in Texas where people have these super-green, really thick, lush lawns. I used to lie on my front lawn, like it was carpet, and look up at the sky. I would lay there for hours sometimes, lost in my thoughts, pondering the deep questions of life. Is God real? Why am I here? What is my purpose? At other times, I would stand in front of the bathroom mirror and have conversations with myself. Staring at my reflection, I would often rhetorically ask myself, "Who are you?"

Even now, after all these years, I can still connect with how those moments of introspection felt. They felt surreal, like I was tapping on the windowpane of another dimension of reality and feeling a bit crazy for doing so. But, truthfully, as far back as I can remember, even when I tried my best to forget, I've always known somewhere deep inside that I was missing something in my life. There had to be *a reason* for my existence. I could feel it.

The emotional pain of not knowing your divine purpose and the accompanying feeling that something is missing in your life is like a much less intense version of the phantom pain people sometimes experience after losing a limb. As horrible as it sounds, it is not uncommon, after having part of an arm or leg amputated, for patients to feel pain or other sensations in the limb that's no longer there. It's most common in arms and legs, but some people will feel it when they have other body parts removed, such as a breast.

Doctors don't know exactly what causes phantom limb pain, but one theory is that your nerves are sending out pain signals because your body senses something is wrong. In the same way, when you don't know the reason for your existence, your spirit sends out emotional pain signals. You are missing something you desperately need, in this case a connection to the Divine and the meaning for your life. But most people are like I was. They either ignore or don't know how to interpret the spiritual signals.

That's **Not It**

When I was younger, I would try to communicate how I felt to others. But people always seemed to attribute the "something missing" in my life to the fact that I was adopted. It was like I was the proverbial adopted kid from a Hallmark movie. You know, the one about the adopted kid who goes searching for their birth parents to fill the emptiness and void they feel in their heart. But, honestly, that was never it for me. I've never felt even a twinge of desire to find my birth parents. Not that there is anything wrong with doing so, I just never felt that way.

Being adopted was never a problem for me; it always felt like a gift. I know that sounds odd. But I think the reason for this has everything to do with the way my mother presented my adoption to me. To this day, I still think it was brilliant and significantly contributed to me feeling precious and unique rather than rejected and abandoned. In fact, my adoption story provided me with such a sense of being special, I can remember wishing everyone could feel the same way. You see, unlike a lot of adopted kids, I always knew I was adopted. And while I don't remember the first time I heard my birth story, I used to ask my mom to tell it to me over and over again. I loved my birth story, which is pretty rare for adopted kids.

The birth story my mom never tired of telling me began with her describing how incredibly desperate she was to have a baby girl. She would always spend a lot of time explaining how her heart was extremely sad before she adopted me because I was missing from her life. Then one day, she would say, "God answered my prayer!" It was time for her to be my mom. So off she went, from hospital to hospital looking for me, searching all over for the perfect little girl. After searching and searching, hospital nursery after hospital nursery, "Voila!" she found me – the perfect baby girl. She would always embellish how incredibly perfect I was, saying, "You were the most perfect baby girl that had ever been born!"

The greatest moment of her life, she would gush, was the moment she laid eyes on me. Instantly she knew. I was *the one*. I was the perfect baby girl her heart had been longing for and she had searched all over to find. It was the happiest day of her life. She would always end with something to the effect of, "Being your mom is the greatest gift I have ever been given." Truthfully, though, this story might be the greatest gift I was ever given. Instead of feeling like being adopted was a curse or cloud that would always be hanging over my head, I believed my life was divinely orchestrated. I even went as far as to feel sorry for other kids who weren't adopted. I would think, "My mamma chose me. Other people just get whatever kid they get."

Of course, at some point, I realized my mom had made the story up. People can't just go into a hospital and pick out their baby after all. But I wasn't angry. I was grateful. I knew it was the reason I had never struggled with being adopted. Looking back, I recognize how deeply this birth story impacted me. I believe it was a huge part of the reason I felt so strongly as a kid that there had to be a reason for my life. I mean, if God went to all the trouble to have me be adopted by my mom, there had to reason *why*. If not, I should have just been "normal" like everybody else.

The Path to Nowhere

As much as I wish I could say my search for significance as a child led me to discovering my life purpose at a young age, unfortunately, that wasn't the case. It would be decades and decades before I would actually discover the *why* of my life. Instead of pressing deeper into the feeling that there was something missing, I ended up following the way of the masses. The path I now call, *The Path to Nowhere*. But, at that time, I didn't even know there was more than one path to take. I just followed the crowd and did the normal thing the majority of people do growing up.

As a teen, like most adolescents, youth culture began to define me. Things like popular opinion, music, my peers, and dating relationships shaped my sense of identity. I had lots of friends. I was a part of *the party crowd.* Fun was pretty much my top priority in life. It was the wild and crazy 80s and I fit the part perfectly. I started doing drugs and abusing alcohol under the guise of fun when I was just 15 years old. Looking back, it was really a way to escape the pain of my home life. Although my adoptive parents loved me very much, their volatile relationship, which led them to divorce when I was in college, made my home life something I wanted to escape. The constant fighting turned violent on more occasions than I can remember. This caused me to step in and assume the role of being my mother's protector. When I graduated high school and went off to college, it was one of the hardest things I had ever done. On one hand, I couldn't wait to leave home and escape the arguing, violence, and chaos, but on the other hand, I was scared to death to leave my mom. Would she be okay without me protecting her? I honestly didn't know.

When I went off to college, the party life I had started in high school grew more reckless and intense. It is a wonder I survived it, honestly. Needless to say, my nonstop partying temporarily snuffed out the questions that seemed to burn so brightly in my heart as a child. I would skip a lot of my classes because I was hung over most mornings. As a result, my schoolwork suffered. I was doing just the bare minimum required to pass my classes. The financial struggle to support my lifestyle made things even worse. I was messed up in so many ways. I lived in survival mode. Without realizing it, I was also using romantic relationships to make myself feel better. I'd had a string of steady boyfriends since the age of fifteen who had been my saviors. They of course didn't recognize the job they were signing up for when they dated me, but those relationships were probably the only thing that kept my sanity intact during this time of my life. Surprisingly, no one, including my boyfriends, really knew how much emotional pain I was in. I'm not even sure I allowed myself to feel it. I was always the life of the party and lots of fun to be around. Like so many comedians who end up self-destructing, humor was one of my most developed survival skills.

Looking back, my college years were really just a blur. Somehow I survived. But the introspective deep-thinking child had morphed into someone I was ashamed to be. I lied almost constantly to keep my life from imploding. One of my lowest points was lying to one of my professors so that he wouldn't fail me for missing so many classes. I had always been really skinny as a kid, so much so that people used to wonder if I was anorexic. Anorexia was just starting to become something more and more people were talking about, and there were several girls on campus pretty much everyone knew were struggling with it.

I knew my parents would kill me if I failed a class. My dad worked incredibly long hours and lots of overtime to put me through college. It was a huge sacrifice for my parents to send me to the private university I attended. So, when my professor confronted me about my excessive absences and poor performance, I lied. I told him I was going home on weekends to pursue counseling for "my eating disorder." His disdain toward me immediately turned to compassion, and our conversation went from him explaining how he was going to fail me to him asking me how he could help me. I remember leaving his office thinking, "I'm definitely going to hell now."

I could probably write several best-selling screenplays about the crazy things my friends and I did in college, but I'll save that for another time. Suffice it to say, I was about as close to knowing my purpose in life when I graduated college as the East is from the West. I had even chosen my major on a whim, thinking my choice would lead to making a lot of money, because I was tired of never having any.

After college, I landed my first *real* job as an accountant and, much to my parents' delight, became self-sufficient. My stint as an accountant didn't last very long, although I was actually pretty good at it. It didn't fit my personality at all. But it did help me find my niche in software sales, selling accounting software to Fortune 500 companies. I was a natural at sales and my career took off. By the age of 25, things were firing on all cylinders career-wise. I had risen to the position of vice president at the second largest software company in the world, making mid-six figures. My days of financial struggle were over and I really enjoyed my job. It was during these early years of success that I married my college sweetheart, and we began to build a life together. We bought our first house and then our second one, enjoying the fruits of our labor.

Although I was successful in many ways, I was really just sleepwalking through life. I was traveling nonstop for my job. It wasn't uncommon for me to be working in a different city every day of the week. On the weekends, I continued to party just as hard as I was working. But through it all, I just couldn't shake the feeling that something was missing. Nothing I accomplished seemed to satisfy me. No matter how many seven-figure deals I closed, or how many exotic vacations my husband and I took, or how many houses we bought, or how many friends we had, deep down inside something was gnawing at me. Another trip, more money, nice material possessions, and career success felt immensely shallow and unfulfilling. However, I had no idea how to connect to a deeper purpose. I still didn't have answers to the questions that I had asked as a child lying on my front lawn looking up at the sky.

Wake-Up Call Number One

But then one day, out of the blue, something horrible happened. My life was unexpectedly interrupted and irrevocably changed forever. It was the first in a series of *wake-up calls* that would drastically shift the direction my life was headed. During the middle of the night, my husband received the news. His mother had a heart attack and passed away. The news shook us both to the core. We were in our twenties. This was not supposed to happen. Up until that time, besides my grandmother's passing when I was around ten, I had never lost anyone close to me. Losing my husband's mother, whom I loved very much, caused all of the questions I had spent hours thinking about as a child to come crashing back into my head.

For the first time, really in my whole life, I came face to face with the fragility of life. It hit me like a ton of bricks. We are all going to die! Until then, the thought had never occurred to me. But now, it was all I could think about. My mother-in-law's sudden passing in the middle of the night made the saying "We aren't promised tomorrow" very real. The prospect of my own death terrified me on so many levels. But at the deepest level, my greatest fear was beginning to surface. What if I reached the end of my life without ever knowing the reason I had lived? I desperately did not want to have lived my life in vain.

Losing a loved one has a funny way of making you think thoughts you would rather avoid. The things I had been taught growing up in church about the afterlife, hell, and Jesus flooded my mind. Yet my own relationship with God was nonexistent. Until then, I had no interest in and didn't think about my relationship with God. I actually hated Christians. I thought they were a bunch of holier-than-thou phonies. But funerals have a way of getting you think about a lot of things. I began to ponder the meaning of life and eventually my thoughts turned toward God. Slowly, it dawned on me. I didn't really know what I believed. I knew the things I had been taught about God in church and, if things came to push or shove, I would have said I believed in God. But did I really? I didn't know what I believed – about my life, about God, about anything, it seemed.

Wake-Up Call Number Two

As all of this was stirring in my heart, my husband and I had the opportunity to get away and take a trip to Europe. I had won a sales award trip at work, and needless to say, it was a welcome distraction. During the trip, while on a train ride between Paris and London, I experienced my second wake-up call. Again, it was pretty much out of the blue. My husband really never read books, but for some reason on this trip, he was reading a book about the events surrounding the O. J. Simpson trial. The book was obviously written by an atheist, because nestled in the middle of the book was a chapter entitled, "God, Where Are You?" After reading this chapter on the train ride, my husband handed me the book, asked me to read it as well, and to tell him what I thought about it.

The chapter he wanted me to read described the reaction of Nicole Brown Simpson's family when the not-guilty verdict was read aloud in the courtroom.

It was common knowledge how the family felt about the verdict. But the book really focused in on what one of the family members spoke out as the verdict was read. Apparently, it was loud enough for everyone to hear. As the verdict was read by the jury, someone from the family blurted out, "God, where are you?" This statement appeared to impact the author so much; he dedicated an entire chapter to it. He used the statement and the fact that innocent people had been brutally murdered to make the point that God couldn't possibly exist. As an attorney himself, the author then went on to make one of the best arguments I had ever heard against the existence of God. As I read the chapter, I could feel my face turning red. For some reason, his argument was making me angry. I mean, really angry.

After I finished reading the chapter, I practically threw the book back at my husband, saying, "That is total BS." I then proceeded to tell my husband all the reasons why there *absolutely was* a God and exactly what I thought about this author for suggesting there wasn't. But, as I defended God with everything in me as we glided across the gorgeous French countryside, I realized I didn't believe a word I was saying. It was awful. In that moment, for the first time in my life, I admitted what I was terrified to admit. The only reason I said I believed in God was that I was afraid to not believe in Him. I had absolutely no grounds for my own faith. I had no firsthand knowledge of Jesus. All I had was the things I had been taught by my parents and others growing up. It was terrifying, honestly. You see, when you grow up in what is referred to in the United States as the *Bible Belt* like I did, you tend to hear a lot about hell. If you don't believe in Jesus, you're going to hell. If you don't live right, you're going to hell. If you don't (fill in the blank), you are going to hell. Everyone has an opinion on hell and they seem to delight in sharing it with you.

As a kid, this terrified me. I didn't want to go to hell. Heck, I just wanted to go outside and play. Yet I remember having dreams about the rapture, being left behind, and not being able to find my parents. Honestly, all that hell business made me afraid *not* to believe in Jesus. I didn't want to go to hell. But, frankly, it also made me afraid *to* believe in Jesus. If Jesus was the kind of guy who sent you to a place where you were burned alive without ever really dying for all of eternity if you chose not to follow Him, He seemed pretty scary to me. I definitely didn't want to follow Him, but I was even more scared not to follow

Him. But I was just a kid. What did I know? Who was I to question God, my parents, and the other grown-ups at church?

I was in a pickle and, like most kids who try to please their parents and stay out of trouble, I decided to "follow Jesus." Or so I thought. In an instant, all of this became crystal clear to me that day on the train to London. What started out as a pretty normal vacation became another defining moment in my life. Thankfully, I made a very important decision on the train that day. I decided to stop believing in God out of fear. I was going to discover my own answers. If the truth ended up being that God didn't exist, well, so be it. Plus I figured if God really existed, surely He was big enough to reveal Himself to me.

After returning from the trip, things really began to unravel. I was still reeling from losing my mother-in-law and the revelation that I didn't really believe in God. Inwardly and outwardly, my life was spinning out of control. Both my husband and I were partying more than ever. I ended up making some really stupid decisions. As a result, my marriage was rapidly disintegrating. It was during this time that I began to see a therapist. I knew something had to change. Depression, anxiety, guilt, shame, and self-hatred were my constant companions. I knew I needed help and, secretly, I wanted permission to divorce my husband. I naively thought he was the source of all my problems, not realizing that his mother's death had uncorked a decade of denial and the underlying reasons why I had been escaping my life with drugs, alcohol, and romantic relationships in the first place.

I look back at this time in my life with so much regret and sorrow. I hurt so many people with the decisions I made and destroyed so many precious relationships. Even though I might have been a bit wild and crazy, I was loved and respected by a lot of wonderful people. Leaving my husband, divorcing him, and making the choices I made during this time were extremely confusing to those closest to me and I completely understand why. No one, including me, realized the depth of pain I was masking with money, drugs, and alcohol. Everyone I knew drank. Most people I knew did drugs. Yes, even the successful ones. And I didn't fit the profile of an alcoholic. I wasn't drinking or doing drugs at work, or going to jail, or losing everything in the traditional sense that you think of when you think of addicts. So no one in their wildest dreams considered me a junkie or alcoholic. We were just *partying like rock stars*. Truthfully, if I had a problem with my partying, then it would have pretty much meant everyone else did too.

Although this time in my life is without a doubt the most out of control, it was also the most enlightening. In therapy, for the very first time I was giving myself room to feel and say things that I needed to feel and say. I was connecting with what was going on inside of me and learning maybe, just maybe, it was possible to find answers to the questions I needed to ask about my life. This was also the first time in well over a decade that I began to give myself permission to consider letting God back into my life. As a result, it wasn't long before I experienced another wake-up call.

Wake-Up Call Number Three

The third wake-up call happened during one of my therapy sessions. But unlike the other two wake-up calls I had experienced, this one actually jarred me out of the daze that I'd been living in for so long. I finally realized what I was missing. I had been asleep to the reason for my existence and the true meaning of my life. I had been sleepwalking through life, going through the motions, year after year, without a sense of direction or a compass that pointed toward true north – the meaning of my life.

I remember the experience like it was yesterday. As I was talking to my therapist, the strangest feeling overtook me. It was like watching myself star in a movie called "My Life." As I observed myself, it was an instantaneous knowing – I was living someone else's life or at least living and acting like a make-believe version of myself. It was a bit like the movie *The Matrix* when Neo takes the red pill. I realized the version of myself and the life I had created were all wrong. I was the leading star in the wrong movie. The character I was playing, the story line, the plot, and how the movie was going to end were totally *off*. In that instant, I knew I had no idea who I was, *really*. I had no idea what my life was supposed to be about. It was terrifying and exhilarating all at the same time.

Getting Honest with Myself and God

After I left the therapy session, on the way home I couldn't stop thinking about what had just happened. I remember praying, "God, you have to help me. I have no idea what the next step should be." I didn't know how to untangle myself from the life I had created. As thankful as I was to be awake in that moment, I recognized that pretty much everyone I knew was in the same boat without realizing it. I couldn't think of a single person who could help me. I didn't know anyone who I felt really knew who they were or was clear about the reason they were on the planet. As a result, I made one of the most important decisions of my life. As the veil was lifted and I realized I had built my life around a false identity and had no idea who I was or how to figure it out, I made a decision. I would make it my life's purpose to find my life's purpose until I found my life's purpose. With laser-like focus, I would search for my life purpose like my life depended on it, because for the first time ever, I realized it did.

While it might have been a simple decision to get on the path to discovering who I was and why I was on the planet, the journey to find the path was anything but. While all of us, I believe, know deep down somewhere inside that there is more to life than what we are experiencing, it's not always easy to get off the merry-go-round of life. And while the wake-up calls of life – such as losing a loved one, divorce, or coming face to face with realizing you've been living a lie – are inevitable, it's ultimately up to each of us to stop hitting the snooze button. Although we've all been given the gift of dreams, callings, and genius to be shared with others, the path to discovering true meaning in life is a narrow one. Jesus, I think, said it best.

Small is the gate and narrow the road that leads to life, and only a few find it.
– Matthew 7:14 (NIV)

Love Note from Dad

My Beloved Child,

Your past does not intimidate me. Nothing about you intimidates me. I know everything about you and I still love you more than life itself. This is why Jesus gave His life for you. I love you more than mere words could express. The only way you would ever understand it is to realize the length I was willing to go so that we could become One.

I realize that it may not all make sense to you right now, but it will. I will make the depths of My love known to you. I have been with you every moment of your life, child. Just because you weren't aware of My presence doesn't mean I wasn't with you. Even when you were running away from Me, you were never far from Me. Even then, I was with you. I was running with you, inside of you, and watching over you at the same time, the entire time. My angels protected you and kept you from falling.

My heart ached knowing that you felt so alone at times. This is why I was always trying to wake you up to the reality of My love and indwelling presence. But trust Me, My love; I am going to use everything that you have experienced in your life to reveal My goodness. The good, the bad, the painful, and even the most traumatic things you have experienced are going to be used in the beautiful story that your life is destined to tell. I am a master at making beautiful things out of even the worst tragedies. If you doubt this, simply look at My Son's death and resurrection. What looked hopeless became the Source of hope. What appeared to be death became the path to Life. The story of your life is not over in fact, it is just beginning. Your most glorious days are ahead. The best is yet to come.

Kisses from Heaven,
Dad

Digging Deeper Exercise 1 - Make Your Purpose to Find Your Purpose

The first step to finding your purpose in life is to make a quality decision to do so. In this next exercise, you are going to make one of the most significant decisions of your life. You are going to partner with God and ask Him to help you make finding your purpose your purpose until you find it.

STEP 1 - Get Alone with God

For this first step, you are going to find a place where you can be completely alone with God. Don't be surprised if you feel led to go somewhere specific. He led Moses to a burning bush and spoke to Gideon beneath a tree. Follow the Holy Spirit's lead and go where you feel led to go. Bring your journal, a blank sheet of paper, and a pen with you.

STEP 2 - Declare Your Intent

Once you get to where you feel led to go, take a moment to acknowledge the holiness of this moment. You are about to set both feet firmly on The Path. Then, when you are ready, speak the following declaration out loud with gusto!

Today, I, (insert your name), make a quality decision to make finding my purpose my life purpose until I find it. God, I invite you to set me firmly on The Path. Lead and guide me into all truth. I give you permission to orchestrate divine circumstances, give me dreams, and open my eyes so that I can discover my divine purpose in life. I receive your dreams and vision for my life. By faith, I declare that I am a person of purpose. I clearly know and understand my purpose and am pursuing it wholeheartedly, by the grace of God. In Jesus' name – AMEN!

STEP 3 - Make It Official

Afterward, copy the declaration in your journal. Then sign and date the statement. Don't skip this important step. There's something significant about signing your name that makes it official. I believe your decision was recorded in heaven and, as a result of your decision, all of heaven is getting involved in helping you find your purpose. You are going to want to remember this day. It will end up being one of the most significant turning points in your life.

CHAPTER THREE

Answering the Wake-Up Call

Waking up from a deep sleep, I always seem to be discovering life for the first time.
– Marty Rubin

The day that I made the decision to make finding my life purpose my life purpose until I found it was a huge turning point in my life. I exited the road that was leading nowhere to embark on a journey to find myself and my true life story. I had no idea where this journey would lead me, but I knew I was finally heading in the right direction. Wake-up calls enter our lives in a variety of different ways. Sometimes they happen through the tragic things we experience and sometimes they are subtler. Rarely do we expect to get these calls. They usually come just as any other wake-up call – as an interruption that jolts us awake.

After the experience I had in my therapist's office – that left me feeling like I was living in a version of my life that didn't fit who I was born to be – things began to happen pretty quickly. At the time, I was in a relationship that needed to end for a variety of reasons. But I had yet to develop enough inner gumption to do what was best for me just because it was best for me. Thankfully, though, when you make a decision to pursue your life purpose, God gets involved in a big way. Within a few months, I was offered an amazing career opportunity to be a part of a software start-up company. It was during the dot-com boom of the early 2000s and the way it came together made it rather obvious that it was *divinely* orchestrated. I was going to have to relocate to Chicago, which I had recently "just so happened" to visit for the first time.

My love affair with Chicago started the moment I touched down at O'Hare Airport. I had the weirdest, most pleasant feeling when I exited the plane. You know how after you've been traveling for a while, how good it feels to get back home? Well, I felt that way when I landed in Chicago. Even thought it was my first trip to Chicago and I had never even been at O'Hare before, it felt like I was arriving home. It was so strange. Then, the city itself felt so alive. I felt so alive. It was just so different from Dallas, where I had grown up. Honestly, it felt just like the fresh start I needed.

Getting the Message Loud and Clear

Over the weekend, some other really unusual things happened. At one point, I was discussing my love of Chicago with a group of friends and rhetorically asked, "Do you think I should move here?" Then, just at that moment a gust of wind came out of nowhere and caused the umbrella we were sitting under to be lifted up and then crash right next my seat. Right at that moment, a very loud thought entered my mind. "What am I going to have to do? Hit you over the head to get the point?" Now, I realize Chicago is the Windy City, but the timing was just too coincidental. I still didn't know how to hear God or have a real conversation with Him. Most of my prayers at this point involved me doing all the talking. I had yet to realize that God's thoughts sounded like mine a lot of the time and didn't recognize that He was speaking to me through my mind. But the umbrella situation, the at-home feeling, and several other strange coincidences were enough to convince me that God was leading me to move to Chicago. Plus, I knew in my heart that moving away was the only way I would have the courage to get out of the relationship I was in and face the things about myself that needed to change.

By this time, I was in my early 30s and I had never really been alone. All the therapy I was doing helped me realize the unhealthy way I used relationships to escape pain. But I was petrified, honestly, to make the move alone. Thankfully, another divine coincidence came together at just the right moment. A really good friend of mine decided they needed a change as well and ended up also moving to Chicago at the same time. I don't know if I would have been able to make such a huge change without her moving as well. She was a Godsend, one of many, that I would experience as I started making finding my true self and my divine purpose my priority.

Coming to the End of Myself

The first few months in Chicago were incredibly hard. Without a relationship to distract me, I turned the party up another notch. That first year in Chicago remains the most difficult time of my life until this day. I met amazing people, had an amazing job, and lived in an amazing city. It should have been a dream come true. But in many ways it felt like a nightmare. I had yet to discover the secret that would ultimately heal my heart and propel me into a life I loved. I was extremely depressed, paralyzed by anxiety, and terribly lonely, even though I was rarely alone. I was drinking pretty much every day to deal with my internal world and feelings of hopelessness. Honestly, I think the worst kind of loneliness on the planet is the kind where you are surrounded by exciting people doing exciting things but inside feel completely alone.

Looking back, God was doing something powerful in my life. I didn't know it at the time, but He was leading me to the end of myself. Although I desperately wanted to discover my life purpose, I was missing the most important thing I needed to discover it – an intimate relationship with Him. But, like most things you don't know that you don't know, it can sometimes take a while to catch a clue. In my mind, I had moved to Chicago to start over, but changing your geographic location is not the key to finding yourself – Jesus is.

> *If you cling to your life, you will lose it;*
> *but if you give up your life for me, you will find it.*
> Matthew 10:39 (NLT)

This scripture is one of the most powerful things Jesus ever said about finding your true life. In the therapist's office, it became clear that I was living in the wrong version of my life, but I didn't know the path to finding the right one. It never occurred to me that Jesus was the way to finding my life. And, honestly, even if it had, I'm not sure I would have been ready to fully surrender to Him. I still had too many religious ideas about what it meant to follow Jesus and live as His disciple. I was still detoxing from the "scary Jesus" of my childhood. Honestly, if I'd thought about it too long, the idea of losing my life for Jesus would have probably turned my stomach. I had no interest in being scared into a relationship with God. And I didn't want to be anything like the religious Christians I had known all my life. To me, they just seemed like the biggest hypocrites in the world. I was beginning to open my heart to Jesus, but as for His followers, no thanks.

I was clueless about so many things during this time in my life. I had so many misconceptions about what it meant to be in a relationship with God. But the crazy thing about being clueless is that rarely do you know you are clueless. You think your experiences and opinions are the only ones. Your truth becomes *the truth*. Personally, I believe being clueless is one of the worst kinds of deception. You don't know what you don't know, and as result you don't realize you're completely deceived. Thank goodness, none of this is a problem for God. He knew exactly where I was and exactly what I needed. The last wake-up call had awakened me enough to get me moving, but I still wasn't fully awake.

Standing at the Crossroads

I remember the moment that everything changed in my life like it was yesterday. Even though I was in a very dark place that first year in Chicago, God was wooing me the whole time. I had met a really lovely Christian who kept pursuing me. She wasn't like a lot of the Christians I had met in my life. She didn't have a judgmental bone in her body. She would hang out with all of us "heathen" and go out with my crazy friends and me on the weekends. She kept asking me to go to church with her, but I never would. She thought I would really like the pastor at the church she attended because he had been an executive at IBM before starting a church. She felt I would be able to relate to him. But I never would go to church with her because I was usually too hung over on Sunday morning to get out of bed.

However, she did tell me about this conference that was going to be in Chicago. The speaker was a woman who had survived all kinds of abuse as a child. I had a couple of her books I had picked up while I was in therapy and they had really spoken to me. I didn't know my decision to go to that conference was going to be the catalyst that would change everything. But it did. I remember walking into the conference and feeling so out of place. I wasn't accustomed to worshipping God with thousands of people and it all seemed so weird. But when the speaker opened her mouth, it was like she was talking directly to me. During the last session, she began to share about what it means to surrender your life to God and be filled with His Spirit. She spoke of something called the baptism of the Spirit and the power of God to live supernaturally.

As she was speaking, something incredible happened. I had a vision. I didn't know anything about visions or really what was even happening to me, but I saw myself standing at a fork in the road. As I was standing there peering down these two paths, I heard a voice speak a scripture to me that I vaguely remembered hearing somewhere before.

Today I have given you the choice between life and death, between blessings and curses. Now I call on heaven and earth to witness the choice you make. Oh, that you would choose life, so that you and your descendants might live!
– Deuteronomy 30:19 (NLT)

As I heard these words, I knew I had a choice to make. Which path would I choose? Looking back, I realize this vision represents where all of us at some point in our lives will find ourselves. As I peered down the road on the left, I knew it was the road that led to death. It was the path I had been on all my life. I could clearly see how my future would look if I continued down this road. It was a path that would lead me to a life tormented by mental illness. If I kept heading down this road, eventually I would end up in a mental institution, out of my mind.

That may seem a bit far-fetched when you look at me today, but at the time, it was very possible. In fact, just a few days before the conference I had been under so much pressure and feeling so anxious and depressed, I was thinking about how nice it would be to go to a mental institution for a while. I thought it would be like a vacation from life. I wouldn't have to worry about my life for a minute. I would be taken care of and could finally rest.

However, in that moment, I saw it for what it was, the path of death. If I chose to go down it, mental illness would steal my mental health and my divine destiny. Totally disturbed by what I was seeing, I decided to look down the other road, the one to the right of the fork in the road. I instantly understood this road to be the road to life. It represented God's plan for my life. But unlike the road to death, I couldn't see where the end of this road led. Everything down this road was blurry. It was then that I heard Deuteronomy 30:19 again. I knew the voice was God and that He was asking me to make a choice. Which road would I choose? I remember thinking at the time, what kind of choice is this? Of course, I don't want to be crazy and lose my mind. Death or life? That seems like a pretty obvious choice. "I choose life," I said softly under my breath. Then the vision ended.

Right at that exact moment, I heard the speaker begin to describe what surrendering your life to Jesus actually looks like. She likened it to Jesus handing you a blank sheet of paper that represented your life and then asking you to sign it. Your signature meant you were giving Jesus permission to write the story of your life however He wanted to write it. You were surrendering to His version of your life instead of the one you had been writing. Finally, I was hearing the answer to the question, "How do I find my life purpose and get from the wrong version of my life to the right one?" As I reflected on the vision I had just experienced, it all seemed so simple and clear. I just needed to choose life. I mean, who in their right mind would choose death? But then again, staying in my right mind had been the battle of my life.

The Moment of Surrender

After the conference ended, I went home and did something a little crazy. I *was* a little crazy though, so it made sense to me at the time. I got a blank piece of paper and signed my name at the bottom of it. I then took the paper into my bedroom and took off all my clothes. I laid face down on the floor with the piece of paper out in front of me and told Jesus he could have me, have my life, and have my future. I remember apologizing because I knew I had nothing to offer to Him except myself. I had made a mess out of my life and I needed him to tell me who I was and what my life was supposed to be. I also remember apologizing for taking so long to get to this place. I felt like I had searched under every rock looking for a solution to my brokenness without being willing to come to Him. I searched so hard for another way that I looked under some of those rocks dozens of times. I admitted that I hadn't wanted to come to Him, because I wanted control. I had decided to pursue other "spiritual paths" because I wanted to be in control of my life. I didn't like the idea of surrender. I had been controlled as a child and it was awful. Plus, I was afraid to trust Him and I didn't think I'd like whatever He wanted my life to be. But, regardless, I was here now, naked as a jaybird, saying, "I give up. You can have my life. You can have me."

I remember at the time thinking how pathetic I was and wondering whether God could even do anything with the likes of me. I was so aware of how I had literally nothing to give Him to work with. I mean, what can you give God, really? After laying there a while in the dark silence, I got up, put my clothes back on, and went and had a glass of wine. I remember feeling peaceful but also a bit apprehensive. I'm not sure what I had expected to happen, but I think I thought I'd feel completely different immediately. But little did I know how much my life was about to change. My decision that day was the spark that would set my heart ablaze with an unquenchable desire to get to know God. And getting to know God is exactly what started to happen.

The Breakthrough

God has a sense of humor. A few days after my naked-surrender-to-God experience, I was walking inside my house when I heard what I now know was the Holy Spirit more clearly than I ever had in my life. What He spoke wasn't what I would have expected to hear. In fact, it made me laugh out loud. He said, "You've got more problems than a math book." Bam, the God of the Universe had spoken to me. I had to laugh. It was funny, really, God telling me the obvious. Then after a few minutes, He continued. "And you can't solve them all at once."

I then saw this picture in my mind, which I would later learn was a Holy Spirit–inspired imagination, of this rubber band ball. You know the ones you can buy at the office supply store? It's literally a ball of rubber bands. Sometimes the rubber bands are rainbow colored and sometimes they are just plain brown ones.

The ones I saw were the rainbow ones. I wasn't sure what it meant at first, but then slowly it dawned on me. I knew it was a picture of my mind. Each one of the rubber bands represented something I believed about myself. In the center of the rubber bands, there was a ball they were all wrapped around. The ball in the center represented who I really was at my core. All the rubber bands were wrapped around me tightly, concealing my true identity.

I then heard the Holy Spirit say, "I know how each of these rubber bands got wrapped around you. I know the order in which they were wrapped around you and I also know the order in which they need to be removed. I am going to set you free." At the time, I didn't have a grid for any of this. I had never heard God so clearly before and I didn't know the Bible well enough to understand how He was giving me a picture of what mind renewal looks like. But it didn't matter that I didn't have a grid for it. What mattered was that I was finally hearing God clearly! I was 33 years old before I heard God's voice for certain. No, it wasn't an audible voice. It was more like a really loud voice in my head. There was also this knowing that is hard to describe. You just *know* it is God. Needless to say, I was pretty excited. For the first time in a really long time, I felt hopeful. It was also really comforting to know that I wasn't going to have to get myself out of the mess I'd made of my life. God was going to lead the way.

I spent the next several months reading every book I could get my hands on about the Holy Spirit, hearing God's voice, and supernatural Christianity. It was like a whole new world had been opened up to me. As a result, things started happening quickly. I learned how to communicate with God and hear from Him myself. I was experiencing God for the first time in my life and He was changing me. I felt like the woman who met Jesus at the well and who was offered living water. Although Jesus knew everything about me, He wasn't rejecting me, He was setting me free!

Getting to know God for myself changed everything. He was nothing like I had been taught growing up. He was the kindest, most gentle, most loving person I had ever met. He was better than I could have ever imagined. His words became my lifeline. Now, instead of doing all the talking when I prayed, I was having two-way conversations and filling up journal after journal with the things He was speaking to me. It was awesome. I also began to regularly have internal visions of Jesus. I didn't know that imaginary prayer was scriptural. I just knew every single encounter with Jesus was life-changing. He was healing my heart and teaching me to see myself from His perspective. In the process, I began to realize just how much I had been missing out on my whole life by not knowing how to communicate with God. Hearing from God and experiencing Him on a daily basis is what normal Christianity actually looks like. Why had no one ever told me that? I had wasted so much time. I had been taught so many stupid things about God. It was like I'd heard bad rumors about God my whole life, and when I finally met Him for myself, I was shocked. So shocked, in fact, I realized somewhere along the way that I didn't want anyone to have to ever experience what I had gone through. If I had hated religion before I met Jesus, I was fit to be tied after hanging out with Him.

Learning to Experience God

From the very first time I heard God's voice, I was hooked. There's simply nothing else in the universe like hearing the voice of Love Himself. And, honestly, for me, if I hadn't heard His voice for myself, I am convinced I would not have been able to believe the scripture that tells us God is Love. Nor would I have known the power of perfect love. Parental love is wonderful. Romantic love is beautiful. The love of friends and family is a huge blessing. But there's nothing that compares to God's perfect love.

Anyone who does not love does not know God, because God is love.
– 1 John 4:8 (ESV)

There is no fear in love, but perfect love casts out fear. For fear has to do with punishment, and whoever fears has not been perfected in love.
– 1 John 4:18 (ESV)

Perfect love is one-way love. It flows from God's heart because of who He is. It isn't based on anything that we do or don't do. It's 100% unconditional. There's no one else besides Love Himself that loves us perfectly. Until you experience it for yourself, it's almost impossible to describe. There is absolutely zero fear, intimidation, manipulation, or control mixed in with God's love. There are no consequences in your relationship with God, no matter how horribly you act up. He's never going to walk out on you, stop talking to you, or try to coerce you into changing to please Him. But you absolutely have to experience it for yourself. Otherwise, by default it seems unbelievable, like there has to be a catch somewhere. No one loves anyone perfectly with zero conditions, right?

Growing up, I was always afraid of God. I thought He was like the controlling authority figures in my life, easily angered and impossible to please. This is probably the main reason I never pursued a relationship with Him. However, nothing could be further from the truth. 1 Corinthians 13, referred to as the love chapter in the Bible, is a beautiful description of God's perfect love.

> *Love is patient and kind. Love is not jealous or boastful or proud or rude. It does not demand its own way. It is not irritable, and it keeps no record of being wronged. It does not rejoice about injustice but rejoices whenever the truth wins out. Love never gives up, never loses faith, is always hopeful, and endures through every circumstance.*
> – 1 Corinthians 13:4–7 (NLT)

Because of my religious upbringing, I thought 1 Corinthians 13 was the description of how I was supposed to love other people. Whenever I read it, all I could think about was how impatient I was, how jealous I was at times, and how rude I could be with others. I completely missed the point. God is patient and kind. God is not jealous, or boastful, or proud, or rude. God does not demand His own way. He's not irritable and keeps no record of wrongs. God rejoices in the truth and never gives up, never loses faith, and is always hopeful. God's love endures through every circumstance. But perfect love is not just something God does, it is who He is.

But, truthfully, I could have read this scripture a million times and never grasped God's love. And it surely never would have been enough for someone to just tell me about God's love. I needed to experience it for myself, as does everyone. The presence of Love, which is God Himself, is what casts out fear. Love is not a theory. Love is meant to be experienced. Even in our human relationships, love is tangible. It can be felt, it can be communicated, and it can be experienced. The Apostle Paul agrees. In Ephesians 3:16–20, Paul explicitly prays that the recipients of his letter would experience God's love.

May He grant you out of the riches of His glory, to be strengthened and spiritually energized with power through His Spirit in your inner self, [indwelling your innermost being and personality], so that Christ may dwell in your hearts through your faith. And may you, having been [deeply] rooted and [securely] grounded in love, be fully capable of comprehending with all the saints [God's people] the width and length and height and depth of His love [fully experiencing that amazing, endless love]; and [that you may come] to know [practically, through personal experience] the love of Christ which far surpasses [mere] knowledge [without experience], that you may be filled up [throughout your being] to all the fullness of God [so that you may have the richest experience of God's presence in your lives, completely filled and flooded with God Himself].
– Ephesians 3:16–20 (AMP)

Verse 19 is where the point really hits home. Here, Paul is praying that these believers would come to know practically, *through personal experience*, the love of Christ. But how can you experience the love of someone you can't hear, see, touch, or smell? You can't. You can't experience the love of someone you don't know personally. This is why learning to use your spiritual senses to experience God is so very, very important. It's also why helping people to encounter God is one of my greatest joys in life. There's nothing quite like seeing the expression on someone's face when they experience God for the first time. It never gets old.

Going to Breakfast with Jesus

Developing a relationship with God is a lot like developing a relationship with anyone else. It requires that you spend time with Him, talking together, hanging out, and just enjoying each other's company. Religion is exhausting. Its voice is always whispering in your ear a list of dos and don'ts and telling you what you should and could be doing. It is never pleased, because there's always more to do and a better way to do it.

But, beloved, this is not the voice of God. God is first and foremost relational! He created human beings for intimacy, love, and fellowship. He longs to reveal Himself to you and for you to get to know Him better. He wants to spend time with you – not just doing what you consider "spiritual" things but also doing fun things and everyday things.

When I first started getting to know God, I would go to breakfast with Jesus. Now, I realize that this may seem strange, but regardless, it was powerful. I would take my journal with me and, as I ate my breakfast, I would write in my journal, talk with Jesus in my thoughts, and imagine Him eating breakfast with me. I would always receive such amazing revelations during these times. And as I began to become more accustomed to using my spiritual sense of touch, I could sense His manifest presence with me. Truthfully, it is wonderful to hang out with Jesus.

It's also amazing, and very important, to overcome the religious tendencies that we all have to make our relationship with God about "doing something" for Him rather than "abiding" in Him. Learning to just sit quietly with God and rest in His loving presence – where there's no agenda except experiencing God in a greater way – will transform your life. While this might seem foreign and feel completely uncomfortable at first – especially since most of us are running at 90 mph most days – let me assure you: Learning to experience God and his manifest presence is one of the most life-giving and productive ways we can spend our time.

Time spent with God is supernaturally refreshing and strategic. He always knows exactly what we need when we need it. He is the most positive, encouraging Person who has ever existed or will exist. You always leave His presence more encouraged, strengthened, and peaceful.

Using Your Spiritual Senses

The good news is that experiencing God is actually much easier than you might think. Every person on the planet has the equipment they need; they just need to learn how to use it. Humans, as both physical and spiritual beings, inherently possess the ability to experience the physical and spiritual realms, and hence experience God. Just like we have five physical senses that enable us to sense and interact with the physical world, we also have five spiritual senses that enable us to sense and interact with the spiritual world. Learning how to activate and use our spiritual senses is *the key.*

It is wrongly assumed by many that when people in the Bible experienced God, it was an external experience that people perceived using their physical senses. In the majority of cases, there is nothing that indicates this to be the case. God's ordinary means of communication, both in biblical and modern times, is spiritual, which means internal. In other words, it's by listening to thoughts and engaging your imagination. For example, when Samuel heard God calling his name and Eli didn't hear it (1 Samuel 3:2–10), Samuel heard God in his own thoughts. When David had a vision of a man by the Tigris River, he indicated he was the only one who saw it. Those with him remained in the dark (Daniel 10:7). Daniel specifically referred to his visions from God as visions that "passed through my mind" (Daniel 1:1, 15).

These and many other scriptures indicate that hearing God and seeing visions are internal, individual experiences. In other words, your spiritual hearing functions the same way you "hear" your own thoughts, inaudibly and internally. Your spiritual eyesight functions the same way you "see" internal pictures, using your imagination. Your spiritual senses of smell and taste allow you to taste and smell in the realm of the spirit. This happens many times while using your imagination but can also happen at other times. It is not uncommon to smell a foul stench in the presence of an evil spirit or a pleasant fragrance in the presence of an angel or Jesus.

As for your spiritual sense of touch, it's difficult to describe how the manifest presence of God feels until you feel it, because it varies from individual to individual. For some, it may feel like heat that rests on certain parts of their bodies. For others, it may feel like chills. For others, it may cause them to physically shake. There's really no right or wrong way to sense the presence of God. The thing that makes the spiritual sense of touch different from physical touch is that there is no external stimulus that is activating it. You feel something invisible – in this case, God's presence.

Imaginary Prayer

The easiest way to activate and exercises all five of your spiritual senses is to engage in a type of contemplative prayer called *imaginary prayer*. Similar to what I did when I would go to breakfast with Jesus, imaginary prayer is simply engaging your imagination as you commune with God. A healthy, vibrant imagination is crucial to a healthy, vibrant spiritual life. Not only are our imaginations God-given, they are an integral part of the way God created us to think and connect with Him and the realm of the Spirit.

Imaginary prayer has a long and rich history both in the Bible and within church history. The church has always assumed God communicated spiritual truths to people through their imaginations, especially through dreams and visions. Saint Augustine, Catherine of Siena, Julian of Norwich, Teresa of Avila, Ignatius of Loyal, Charles Finney – along with countless others – have shared the revelations they received in imaginary prayer that powerfully impacted their lives. In fact, Saint Teresa called her internal meeting place with God her "interior castle."

In the Digging Deeper Exercise at the end of this chapter, I will walk you step by step through an imaginary prayer example. If you've never done anything like this before, don't worry – it's so easy even children can do it. In fact, a lot of times children find it easier than adults to experience God. They haven't been exposed to as much religious nonsense as we grown-ups. The only thing that really matters is that you experience and hear God yourself. Until you do, not only will you struggle in the quest to discover your life purpose, you will be missing out on knowing the most incredible Person who has ever existed. I realize a lot of people who consider themselves spiritual generically relate to "God" or the "Universe" or a "Higher Being." But there is so much more available to us than this. Experiencing God for who He really is will absolutely blow your mind.

Love Note from God

My Incredible Child,

I've been waiting for this moment for all your life. Come, take My hand, and take a walk with Me down The Path. I want to show you our secret place. Come, sit with Me, and feel the gentle wind of My Spirit blowing all around you. I created this place just for us. I want it to be a safe place for you, beloved. Somewhere you can come anytime you want to just "be" without any fear of judgment, rejection, or condemnation. If you need to talk, I love to listen. If you need something, just ask. If you have questions, I have answers. If you just need to rest, you can lay your head on My chest and listen to My heartbeat. I'll sing you a lullaby and rock you to sleep. Whatever you need, my beloved, is okay with Me. You are free just to be. The only thing I want is to love you the way you need to be loved — the way I created you to be loved.

Sometimes, though, I have to warn you, I may surprise you. I'm much better than you've imagined. My perfect love takes some getting used to. There's nothing you could ever think, say, or do that will ever change my opinion of you. My love for you is settled forever — that's why it's called eternal love. You can talk to me about anything and everything, or if you don't feel like talking, that's okay too. I already know everything about you, so really, you telling Me is optional. Our relationship is not about what you can do for Me. It's about what you need to receive from Me. My perfect love manifests in all kinds of ways. It can be practical or lavishly extravagant. It can be frivolous or serious; it all depends on what you need Me to be at that moment. If all of this sounds too good to be true, then good, it means I'm doing a good job of explaining Myself. "Too good to be true" like a "dream come true" is how perfect love is supposed to feel.

Kisses from Heaven,
Dad

Digging Deeper Exercise – Surrender in the Secret Place

STEP 1 – Scripture Reading

> *He who dwells in the secret place of the Most High,*
> *shall abide under the shadow of the Almighty.*
> *I will say of the Lord, "He is my refuge and my fortress;*
> *My God, in Him I will trust."*
> – Psalms 91:1–2 (NKJV)

This scripture from Psalms 91 speaks of a "secret place" with God where we find refuge and safety. In this exercise, we'll be learning how to create an inner secret place, through the power of imaginative prayer, where we can experience God's presence and learn to rest in His love, grace, and goodness. This may be the very first time you've tried something like this. That is just fine. You are in for a treat. Learning to encounter God and rest in His love is one of the most powerful things in the universe.

We are so accustomed to working, performing, striving, and trying; we often bring this mentality into our relationship with God. But, with God, real power arises from a position of rest, and lasting transformation happens, not because we are trying but through His power and grace. While this may seem strange and unnatural at first, don't worry; most things that are spiritual and supernatural usually feel that way in the beginning.

STEP 2 – Set the Atmosphere

Finding the right location for this exercise is important. You can experiment with several different spots to see what you like best, but here are a few things to consider:

- Find a quiet place where you can be alone with God without interruptions or distractions.
- Set aside enough time. You want to give God your full attention and give yourself enough time so that you aren't feeling rushed.

- Take the time to create a worshipful, peaceful atmosphere. Dim the lights, light a candle, fill the room with flowers, or play soothing music.
- Get comfortable. Wear comfortable clothes, gather pillows and blankets to lie down on, or choose a spot where there's a recliner.

STEP 3 - Prayer to Activate Your Spiritual Senses

Once you have prepared your surroundings, it is time to go inward and commune with the One who loves you like no other. Begin by praying this prayer out loud:

Holy Spirit, I am here today to create a special place in my heart to meet with You and get to know You better. I want to move beyond just knowledge about You into personal experiences with You. I want to develop a deeper, more intimate relationship with You, Jesus, and my Heavenly Father. I want to experience Your kingdom within and experience the fullness of what it means to live in union with You. Sanctify my imagination. Think through my thoughts. Help me tangibly experience You with all five of my spiritual senses. Teach me how to experience You. In Jesus' name, AMEN!

STEP 4 - Go Inward

The next step is to go inward. Using your imagination, picture your own personal secret meeting place with God. Feel free to imagine a place that is special to you. It can be a garden, the top of a mountain, the beach, or a cabin in the woods with a warm fire burning. If you're having trouble imagining a specific place, sometimes the easiest thing is to think of a pleasant memory, an actual place you've been. It doesn't really matter if you've been there or not, as long as it feels special to you.

Remember, the purpose of this exercise is to go inward and create an inner space, a private place where you can meet with and experience God. This is a place where it is completely safe to be you and be totally open and transparent with God. As you practice recalling this place, it's going to become easier and easier to sense God's presence and commune with the Father, Jesus, and the Holy Spirit. The point is to experience God through imaginative prayer. Establishing your internal meeting place is a really important first step. So, go for it. I have seen amazing transformations take place as people begin to experience God in this way.

Once you have an image of the place in your mind, focus intently. Engage all five of your spiritual senses. "Smell" the air, "feel" the breeze, "hear" the sounds around you. Experience this inward place in all of its beauty. Spend as much time as necessary taking in your surroundings, feeling the solitude and serenity of the place. When you feel like you're really engaged, invite God to join you. However He chooses to show up is fine. Take a few moments to notice the details of His appearance. Then, just enjoy His presence. Talk with Him, laugh with Him, cry with Him, and allow him to take you wherever He wants to go.

As you engage in this exercise, recognize how you experience God's presence. Do you feel His peace? Is there a physical manifestation of any kind? The manifest presence of God is tangible; it can be felt physically at times.

STEP 5 - A Moment of Surrender

The wonderful thing about your secret place with God is that, because it's a place you visit in your imagination, you can go there anytime you'd like. In this next step, imagine you are back in your secret place. Except this time, you have brought a blank piece of paper with you. Your goal is to meet with God, hand Him this piece of paper, and give Him permission to use it to write your life story.

Take a moment before you begin to pray the following prayer out loud. As you pray the prayer, feel free to add your own words and pour out your heart.

Father, You knew me before I was born. You know everything about me. You created me for Your purposes. Today I come before You with this blank piece of paper that represents my life. It's blank because You're the author of my life story. My story line has always been Yours to write. Fill in this sheet of paper with the things You've desired and written about me. Divide my life into chapters and seasons as You see fit. Use my body, my mind, my gifts, and my talent – everything that I am – to bless and serve others and glorify You. In Jesus' name, AMEN!

STEP 6 - Sign Your Name

After praying, imagine you are standing before the Father with a blank sheet of paper. Allow the experience to unfold however it happens. When you are ready, sign your name at the bottom of the blank sheet of paper you brought with you and hand it over to the Father, signifying that you are surrendering your life to Him. Then pray the following prayer:

Father, I am signing this blank piece of paper today to signify that I am in agreement with Your divine purpose for my life. I give you permission to cause my life purpose to come to pass in my life. In Jesus' name, AMEN!

STEP 7 - Journal

Afterward, take out your journal and write down your experience as well as your thoughts, emotions, and impressions about your experience.

CHAPTER FOUR

The 1st Big Q: Who Is God?

God save us from religion.
– David Eddings

In the next five chapters, we are going to walk down the path that leads to discovering your life purpose. Along this path, you're going to find your very own God-breathed answers to what I call The 5 Big Qs of Life – *Who is God? Who am I? Why am I here? Where am I headed? How do I get there?* Our adventure over the course of the next five chapters will lead you on an exciting journey of self-discovery and God encounters. Together, we'll head deep into the Father's heart to discover what He dreamed your life would look like when He created you.

The 5 Big Q's of Life are the exact questions Emergers ask and answer in detail while enrolled in Emerge School of Transformation. The reason is simple but profound. Having your own conversations with God about these questions helps you get to know God personally and learn to hear from Him for yourself, which is exactly what you need to discover to fulfill your divine purpose. At the end of each of the next five chapters, the Digging Deeper Exercise will help facilitate conversations between you and God so that you can personally experience His heart for you.

The 1st Big Q, *Who is God?* is first for a reason. It's because who you believe God to be drastically affects how you experience Him and profoundly influences your ability to receive His answers to the other four questions. For example, if you believe God is a distant judge who relates conditionally to people based on their performance and strict adherence to His moral law, you will more than likely experience God as someone who is focused on your mistakes and who makes you feel guilty when you mess up. You'll also probably find it difficult or will even avoid hearing from Him. I mean, who wants to talk to someone who's always focused on the negative? But if you believe God is a patient Father who is lovingly guiding you through painful experiences, helping you forgive and love yourself, and actively involved in your life, you will most likely experience Him as someone you can trust. You'll be eager to talk to Him and feel comfortable asking Him life's most important questions.

If you feel like I did before I developed a personal relationship with God – that His plan for your life is probably going to involve a lot of suffering or revolve around you doing something you would never choose for yourself – you may not be very open to hearing your divine purpose. However, if you've experienced God as someone who always has your back and only wants the very best for you, then you're probably eager to hear from Him about your life purpose. The bottom line is this: The negative filters you view God through affect your relationship with Him. They also hinder your desire and ability to hear from Him. Like a dirty pair of eyeglasses, negative filters obscure God's face and make it hard to see what He's saying.

Will the Real God Please Stand Up?

If we want to see God clearly for who He really is, we need to clean our "eyeglasses," so to speak, and give God a clean slate. All of us have a pair of lenses, or perceptional filters, that we view God through. These lenses were formed over the course of our life as we made various judgments about God. A simple example that shows how perceptional filters influence what we experience and expect is how we view marriage. Your opinion of marriage will vary greatly depending on how you grew up. Were your parents married or divorced? If they were married, were they happily or unhappily married? Did they fight in front of you or did they discuss their disagreements in private?

Whether we realize it or not, our view of marriage is heavily influenced by the way our parents interacted. Most of the time, we are unaware of what we really believe about marriage until we get married. The reason for this is that our true beliefs are held at a subconscious level. This is the reason children from divorced homes typically experience a higher rate of divorce than those who come from homes with married parents. We tend to replicate, as adults, the things that were modeled to us as children. But most don't realize, if ever, they have a "divorce lens" they are viewing marriage through until they've experienced at least one divorce.

In the context of our relationship with God, the same is true. For most of us, there are things we have experienced over the course of our lives that have negatively impacted the way we see God. The judgments we made about those experiences and about God Himself are what distort our image of God and hinder our ability to perceive Him for who He really is. Our family of origin's beliefs about God, our church experiences, our experiences with spiritual people and other world religions, popular culture, our understanding of scripture, our supernatural experiences or lack thereof – these are just a few of the things that influence and shape our perceptual filters and form the lenses that we view God through. It's no wonder that most of us are viewing God through such dirty lenses.

Reimagining Your Image of God

Steve, one of my Emerge students, is a great example of how our image of God is influenced by our past experiences. As a little boy, Steve was told if he waited on God, he would experience God's presence and hear God's voice. So Steve, always one to accept a challenge, went home and tried it. He sat on his bunkbed for what seemed like forever, *waiting on God*. He waited, and waited, and waited. But nothing happened. God didn't show up. He didn't hear God say anything. No voice, no visions, just a blank silence. Needless to say, he was very disappointed. He felt confused and wondered why God didn't show up or want to talk to him. Then without realizing what he was doing, he decided God must not like him. Maybe he was unworthy to talk to God. Maybe there was something wrong with Him. He felt disappointment like he had never felt before. It wasn't the *I didn't get what I wanted for my birthday* kind of disappointment; it was the *I must not have value* level of disappointment. It was a life-defining moment for Steve and his relationship with God. The experience shaped who he thought God was. But it not only caused him to form a distorted image of God, it caused him to form a distorted image of himself. God was a jerk and he was worthless. These core beliefs traveled with Steve his whole life.

As you can imagine, based on what happened, Steve never heard from God until he started Emerge. He had been a Christian his whole life and even went to church on a fairly regular basis. But he was just going through the motions, for the most part. Deep down, he was offended by God. Although he didn't consciously remember the experience he had as a child, it dramatically affected His relationship with God. In Emerge, working through his own answer to the 1st Big Q, *Who is God?*, the Holy Spirit reminded Steve of what had happened to him as a child. As Steve recalled what happened, the pain of the experience came rushing to the surface.

Reliving the memory was extraordinarily painful. But this time Steve was not alone. The Holy Spirit had led him there and was about to remove the perceptional filter that had damaged their relationship. As Steve wept, once again connecting with how he felt as a little boy, the Holy Spirit opened Steve's eyes to the spiritual realm. Suddenly, he could see what was there all along but invisible to his natural sight. The Father was right there with him, lying beside him, cuddling with him. He wasn't speaking; He was silent, enjoying Steve's company. Still startled by the new revelation, he heard the Father speak. "This was Daddy and Steve cuddle time. I miss that a lot." When Steve heard the Father's voice, he was overwhelmed. God had been there the entire time. And not only was He *there*, He actually missed that Steve had stopped waiting on Him.

This experience with God shifted Steve's relationship with God. It reshaped his image of God so that Steve could relate to God as Father. Today, Steve enjoys a level of intimacy with God that he never dreamed possible. This experience also greatly impacted Steve's self-perception. Instead of believing he wasn't valuable, he began to have more self-confidence as he recognized his inherent God-given worth. The powerful experience Steve experienced is one of many examples I could share with you that demonstrate how much our experiences shape our image of God and influence our answer to the question, *Who is God?*

These experiences also prove the importance of encountering God for ourselves. If an original belief about God was formed through an experience, it only makes sense that a new belief about God is most easily formed through a new experience. This is one of the most important reasons so much of my work is focused on helping people encounter God for themselves. When the Holy Spirit transforms a memory by removing the limitation of our physical eyesight so that we can see how God was present, the results are miraculous. Once we are able to perceive God's presence, we can also hear the truth that He wants to speak to us in that moment. Painful memories become peaceful memories as the Holy Spirit transforms our perception of what happened.

Recognizing that we all have perceptional filters is a huge key to experiencing more of God and answering the 1st Big Q. It also helps us develop more self-awareness in other areas of our life. Recognizing our perceptional filters causes us to distrust our own judgments and interpretations of our life experiences. It helps us to rely more on God's interpretation of things. Time and time again, I have seen God shift people's perceptions and help them reinterpret the things they've experienced or, in Steve's case, not experienced. To accurately answer the question, *Who is God?*, it is imperative that we allow Him to remove the perceptional filters that have caused us to have a distorted image of Him.

God's Self-Portrait

If we want to get to know God for who He really is, we need to give Him the opportunity to introduce and define Himself. I'm assuming that if you've made it this far in the book, you are either already a Christian or at least open to Jesus being who He claimed to be – God incarnate, or God in human form. The reason this is important is that understanding who Jesus is, is *huge* if you want to understand who God is. In fact, one of the primary reasons Jesus was manifested as God's Son was to show who God really is. The writers of the gospels as well as Jesus Himself said over and over again in a variety of ways that Jesus *was* the very best representation of God's nature and character. In the book of Hebrews, the author says it this way:

Throughout our history God has spoken to our ancestors by his prophets in many different ways. The revelation he gave them was only a fragment at a time, building one truth upon another. But to us living in these last days, God now speaks to us openly in the language of a Son, the appointed Heir of everything, for

through him God created the panorama of all things and all time. The Son is the
dazzling radiance of God's splendor, the exact expression of God's true nature – his
mirror image! He holds the universe together and expands it by the mighty power
of his spoken word. He accomplished for us the complete cleansing of sins, and
then took his seat on the highest throne at the right hand of the majestic One.
– Hebrews 1:1–3 (TPT)

This scripture explains one of the primary and most important differences between the Old and New Testaments. In the Old Testament, God was speaking to us through people as a way to slowly reveal Himself bit by bit. However, in the New Testament, God's approach shifted. He was now speaking openly to us through Jesus. Jesus is described as God's *mirror image – the dazzling radiance of God's splendor, the exact expression of God's true nature.* The Amplified, Classic Edition translation of Hebrews 1:3 goes as far as to call Jesus "the perfect imprint and very image of [God's] nature."

He is the sole expression of the glory of God [the Light-being, the out-raying or radiance
of the divine], and He is the perfect imprint and very image of [God's] nature.
– Hebrews 1:3a (AMPC)

The book of John, at its outset, provides another fascinating description of Jesus as God. This Gospel begins not with an account of Jesus' birth or John's baptism but with a recounting of the creation story in Genesis. John's description of Jesus as *the Word* who was with God and was God is incredible to really think about. Jesus, as the Word, was with God the Father and was also one with God the Father in the form of the Father's words at the moment He spoke the cosmos into existence.

In the beginning was the Word, and the Word was with God, and the Word was
God. He was with God in the beginning. Through him all things were made;
without him nothing was made that has been made. In him was life, and that life
was the light of all mankind. The light shines in the darkness, and the darkness has
not overcome it.
– John 1:1–5 (NIV)

This idea of Jesus being present with God, as God, at the moment of creation is a bit mind-boggling. But John doesn't stop there. He goes on to say that *the Word* became flesh.

> *The Word became flesh and made his dwelling among us. We have seen his glory, the glory of the one and only Son, who came from the Father, full of grace and truth.*
> – John 1:14 (NIV)

The incarnation of Jesus or Jesus as *the Word* becoming flesh means this – Jesus is God in human form. The Word, which was God in the beginning, became flesh. Even though He is called the Son of God, He is also God the Father.

The Word = Jesus = God the Father

If your head isn't spinning yet, hold on to your horses, there's more. The idea that God the Father and God the Son, that is, Jesus, are one and the same is a concept that runs deep all throughout the New Testament. It actually forms the basis of the doctrine of the Trinity, a three-in-one God, which includes God's Spirit, the Holy Spirit. I'll be tackling the concept of a Triune God, Father, Son, and Holy Spirit, in more detail in just a moment, but for now hang with me. The big point here is that when you see Jesus you are looking at God. Jesus is the exact representation of God's character. When you look at Jesus the Son, He is a perfect reflection of God the Father.

Jesus Is Perfect Theology

Let's take a few moments to break this down a little further. The Apostle John wasn't the only one making the claim that Jesus and the Father were one and the same. Jesus made the claim over and over again Himself.

> *I and the Father are one.*
> – John 10:30 (NIV)

In John 10:30, Jesus makes a blasphemous statement. He confirmed His Deity, saying He and the Father were one. Since we live in modern times, it is sometimes hard to imagine the actual impact this statement had on the audience Jesus was speaking to, unbelieving Jews. There were so many things about this statement that were offensive to them. One, Jesus was making Himself out to be equal with God Almighty, and two, He was calling God *Father* like God was His actual Dad. The Jews clearly understood Jesus' intent. In fact, they were so offended by Jesus' statement, they called him a demon and a madman and even tried to stone Him. If you continue reading, just a little further, in verse 33, the Jewish leaders say, "You, being a man, make yourself God."

Over and over again, Jesus Himself made the claim to *be God* or be *one with God*. But perhaps one of the clearest passages of scripture that describe Jesus as God comes from the book of Colossians.

> He is the divine portrait, the true likeness of the invisible God, and the firstborn Heir of all creation. For the Son created everything, both in the heavenly realm and on the earth, all that is seen and all that is unseen. Every seat of power, realm of government, principality, and authority — it was all created by him and for his purpose! He existed before anything was made, so now everything finds completion in him. He is the Head of his body, which is the church. And since he is the Beginning and the Firstborn Heir in resurrection, he must always be embraced as the most exalted One, holding first place in everything. For God is satisfied to have all his fullness dwelling in Christ.
> – Colossians 1:15–19 (TPT)

This is such a powerful passage of scripture. In it, Jesus is described as God's divine portrait, the true likeness of the invisible God. And then as the most exalted One in Whom God is satisfied to have all His fullness dwelling. It doesn't get much clearer than this. Jesus is God's self-portrait. God looks like Jesus, Jesus looks like God. God acts like Jesus, Jesus acts like God. God speaks like Jesus, because Jesus is God. The Father and Jesus are One! This point is reiterated over and over again all throughout the New Testament. All of these scriptures paint a very clear picture of God. If you want to know who God is and what He's actually like, look no further than Jesus. Jesus is perfect theology.

Detoxing from Religion

If Jesus is perfect theology, then it goes without saying that we need to understand what Jesus is like. But what's the best way to go about that? This has become a real challenge in modern times. There are so many conflicting viewpoints about Jesus. And, sadly, in the American culture where I live, as you develop your relationship with God and get to know what Jesus is really like, you will at some point, more than likely, have to deal with the ways Christianity, as an organized religion, has misrepresented Jesus.

As sad as that statement is, and as hard as it may be for Christians to admit, it needs to be said. If the truth be told, the Christian religion, and for that matter, Christians themselves, especially here in the United States, is probably one of the biggest reasons people struggle to know God for themselves. Unfortunately, a lot of people are like I once was – turned off by Christians. And they want nothing to do with the Jesus these people represent.

Tragically, the reflection of Jesus that most people see when they look at the Western church looks nothing like Jesus at all. As Christians, we are supposed to be known by our love, yet to people who haven't met Jesus for themselves yet, we are known for everything but that. According to polls conducted by David Kinnaman and Gabe Lyons, authors of *unChristian: What a New Generation Really Thinks About Christianity... And Why It Matters,* people who don't know Jesus aren't impressed. These guys spent three years polling young, unchurched Americans to find out what they thought about Christianity. Millions of young people, they discovered, see us as judgmental, hypocritical, anti-homosexual, too political, insensitive – and boring. What's more disturbing is that a shocking 50% of respondents said they base their negative views on personal contacts with Christians, stating, "Many of those outside of Christianity... reject Jesus because they feel rejected by Christians."

This is why so much of my work in Emerge is focused on helping students detox from religion. Their stories vary, but it seems that most all of them have been negatively impacted by Christians or the church in some way. As a result, there are all kinds of misconceptions about God that they are having to overcome.

Branden and his wife Sophia went through Emerge together as a couple. Although lifelong Christians, they had not been to church for over ten years when they joined Emerge. Their family had spent years in what they described as a sin-focused, very controlling church that almost cost them their relationship with God. Thankfully, after years of spiritual abuse, they decided to leave, but the damage was immense.

Being a part of Emerge was a huge turning point for them. As they opened themselves up to truth about who God really is and began to encounter Him for themselves, their hearts began to heal. Furthermore, hearing the gospel as a grace-based, love-infused message rather than a hellfire and brimstone, fear-infused message set their hearts ablaze. But most exciting of all was the transformation that took place in the way they loved other people.

Midway through the program, their daughter became pregnant out of wedlock. Instead of feeling ashamed and judging their daughter, they were able to respond with unconditional love. Their daughter – who was also estranged from God because of their church background – was shocked at their response. Over the course of her pregnancy, her parents continued to bless her and her baby and share with her just how precious both of them were to God. As a result, their daughter opened to developing her own relationship with God.

Unfortunately, stories like Branden and Sophia's are very common. This is why I am so adamant with Emergers that they take the time they need to get to know God for themselves and detox from the fake gospel they've been fed over the course of their lives. Grace and works are like oil and water. They don't mix well at all and they will absolutely poison your relationship with God.

The True Gospel

Jesus didn't come to establish a new world religion. The gospel is about something so much more revolutionary than that. The gospel is the unveiling of a new way of living as one with God "in Christ." Jesus came into the world to re-create our whole world. He came to change our human nature from sinner to saint and our relationship with God so that we no longer related to Him from the outside but from the inside. This is what it means to be "in Christ."

The New Testament is chock full of "in Christ" and union with God scriptures. In fact, we spend a great deal of time in Emerge meditating on them to uproot from people's psyches the illusion of separation from God. Here are a few of my favorites:

My prayer is not for them alone. I pray also for those who will believe in me through their message, that all of them may be one, Father, just as you are in me and I am in you. May they also be in us so that the world may believe that you have sent me. I have given them the glory that You gave me, that they may be one as we are one — I in them and You in me — so that they may be brought to complete unity. Then the world will know that You sent me and have loved them even as You have loved me.
– John 17:20–23 (NIV)

For God wanted them to know that the riches and glory of Christ are for you Gentiles, too. And this is the secret: Christ lives in you. This gives you assurance of sharing his glory.
– Colossians 1:27 (NLT)

But whoever is united with the Lord is one with him in spirit.
– 1 Corinthians 6:17 (NIV)

Don't you realize that your body is the temple of the Holy Spirit, who lives in you and was given to you by God? You do not belong to yourself.
– 1 Corinthians 6:19 (NLT)

There is therefore now no condemnation for those who are in Christ Jesus.
– Romans 8:1 (ESV)

The Spirit of God, who raised Jesus from the dead, lives in you.
– Romans 8:11a (NIV)

For He raised us from the dead along with Christ and seated us with Him in the heavenly realms because we are united with Christ Jesus.
– Ephesians 2:6 (NLT)

Therefore, if anyone is in Christ, he is a new creation. The old has passed away; behold, the new has come.
– 2 Corinthians 5:17 (ESV)

My old identity has been co-crucified with Messiah and no longer lives; for the nails of his cross crucified me with him. And now the essence of this new life is no longer mine, for the Anointed One lives his life through me — we live in union as one! My new life is empowered by the faith of the Son of God who loves me so much that he gave himself for me, and dispenses his life into mine.
– Galatians 2:10 (TPT)

I could go on and on about each one of these scriptures. Being "in Christ Jesus" is such a breathtaking reality. But what's even more breathtaking about our union with God is that it isn't based on anything we do or don't do. It's based on what Jesus already accomplished on the cross!

For it's by God's grace that you have been saved. You receive it through faith. It was not our plan or our effort. It is God's gift, pure and simple. You didn't earn it, not one of us did, so don't go around bragging that you must have done something amazing.
– Ephesians 2:8–9 (Voice)

But what about sin and being a good person or any number of other things people believe impact their relationship with God? That's the thing that makes the gospel almost too good to be true. Our union with God isn't based on anything other than Jesus Christ. Jesus Christ is *the way* to union with God, period. You don't have to do anything except receive it. Just believe it and enjoy it!

I realize there are enormous theological ramifications to an unconditional union with God through Christ. But, if you have a problem with it, recognize your problem is with Jesus and the Apostle Paul. A close examination of the New Testament, especially in the epistles, will confirm just how much time Paul spends explaining our union with God as the whole enchilada of the gospel. He references our union with God no less than 264 times in his writings. Paul's goal, in fact, was to make sure we understood the message of the cross, *Christ in you*, loud and clear. Paul speaks of this new union relationship using several keywords and phrases to describe it such as *in Him, of Him, with Him, through Him, by Him, by Whom, for Him*. All of these variations play a part in explaining Paul's message to us about our union with God.

This is also why I spend a fair amount of time and effort during Emerge unpacking how our union with God changes our understanding of the gospel and most other Christian doctrines. In fact, our union with God should change everything about our relationship with God – the way we worship, the way we pray, and the way we commune with Him. But it's not a simple task to undo, the sometimes decades of religious ideas people have digested about the gospel and their relationship with God. Even people who intellectually agree with the idea of Jesus living in them – and vice versa – rarely experience it or relate to God from this vantage point on a daily basis. Overcoming the illusion from separation from God is something that can take some time, but the results are worth every minute.

Experiencing Jesus' Relationship with the Father

John 14 is one of my favorite passages of scripture. I love the way it explains who Jesus is and how He came to place us smack dab in the middle of His relationship with the Father.

> *Jesus said, "I am the Road, also the Truth, also the Life. No one gets to the Father apart from me. If you really knew me, you would know my Father as well. From now on, you do know him.*
>
> *You've even seen him!" Philip said, "Master, show us the Father; then we'll be content."*
>
> *"You've been with me all this time, Philip, and you still don't understand? To see me is to see the Father. So how can you ask, 'Where is the Father?' Don't you believe that I am in the Father and the Father is in me? The words that I speak to you aren't mere words. I don't just make them up on my own. The Father who resides in me crafts each word into a divine act."*
> *– John 14:6–10 (MSG)*

In verses 6 through 10, Jesus beautifully reveals His purpose – to be the road that leads us to the Father and to be a representation of what the Father is really like. The way that Father looks when you look at Jesus is breathtaking. The Father, like Jesus, isn't sin-obsessed. He's love-obsessed. As you read through the gospels, you learn that Jesus' friends weren't religious goodie-two-shoes kind of folk; they were rejects, outcasts, and the untouchables of His day. The way He treated people was shocking to religious people. Even His disciples weren't religious scholars. They were ordinary guys (Acts 4:13).

> I will not leave you orphaned. I'm coming back. In just a little while the world will no longer see Me, but you're going to see Me because I am alive and you're about to come alive. At that moment you will know absolutely that I'm in my Father, and you're in Me, and I'm in you.
> – John 14:18–20 (MSG)

But in verse 18, things get really interesting. Here, Jesus explains to his disciples what is about to happen to Him. But, more importantly, He also explains what is about to happen to *them*. He's not going to abandon them. He's coming back. And when He does, it's going to be amazing! Through his death and resurrection, His disciples were about to experience the same kind of relationship with God He had. They, too, were going to become one with the Father. They were going to live inside of God and God was going to live inside of them. There would be no more separation from God.

Of course, Jesus' message in John 14 is not only for his twelve disciples but for all of us. Through Jesus, we now live inside of God and God lives inside of us. This is the beauty of the gospel. Separation from God *is* just an illusion. However, this is rarely how the gospel is presented or how Christianity is experienced. This is one of the reasons it took me so many years to become open to having a real relationship with God.

Living in the Father's House

Let's take a few moments to dissect John 14 in a little more detail and grasp the reality of what it means to live in union with the Father.

> "Let not your heart be troubled; you believe in God, believe also in Me. In My Father's house are many mansions; if it were not so, I would have told you. I go to prepare a place for you. And if I go and prepare a place for you, I will come again and receive you to Myself; that where I am, there you may be also. And where I go you know, and the way you know." Thomas said to Him, "Lord, we do not know

where You are going, and how can we know the way?" Jesus said to him, "I am the way, the truth, and the life. No one comes to the Father except through Me."
– John 14:1–7 (NKJV)

I've heard many sermons – and even songs have been written – about verse 2 that say this passage of scripture is referring to these mansions in heaven we're going to live in someday. However, this isn't what Jesus was saying at all. He wasn't referring to the Father's physical house or going away to prepare a physical place for us to live in heaven. He was saying we are mansions who were going to live inside the Father's house, which is the *Father's body.* Jesus was going away to prepare a place *within the Father Himself* for us to live.

Many passages of scripture in the New Testament refer to physical bodies as houses or temples. In John 2:19, Jesus told the Pharisees, "Destroy this temple, and I will raise it again in three days." Jesus wasn't saying to destroy the Temple in Jerusalem; he was referring to His body that was going to be crucified and raised again after three days. In Luke 11:24, Jesus said, "When an evil spirit leaves a person, it goes into the desert, searching for rest. But when it finds none, it says, 'I will return to the person I came from.' So it returns and finds that its former home is all swept and in order." In this instance, Jesus likened a person's body to a house. Another example is found in 1 Corinthians 6:19. It calls our bodies the "temple of the Holy Spirit." From these scriptures and others, we can clearly deduct what Jesus was saying. Jesus is the way for us to live *inside* of the Father.

If you continue reading down a little further in John 14, in verse 19, Jesus further expounds on this new inside-out way of relating to God that his disciples are about to experience.

And I will pray the Father, and He will give you another Helper, that He may abide with you forever – the Spirit of truth, whom the world cannot receive, because it neither sees Him nor knows Him; but you know Him, for He dwells with you and will be in you. I will not leave you orphans; I will come to you. A little while longer and the world will see Me no more, but you will see Me. Because I live, you will live also. At that day you will know that I am in My Father, and you in Me, and I in you.
– John 14:16–20 (NKJV)

Here Jesus explains how this new union relationship with God is going to work. The Holy Spirit would live inside of them (verse 17). Jesus would live inside them (verse 18). They would live inside Jesus (verse 18). Then, through their union with Jesus, they would experience union with the Father. The Father would live inside of them and they would live inside of the Father (verse 20).

Let those words and the reality of what they mean sink in for just a moment. You are one with God through Jesus Christ. You are one with the Holy Spirit, you are one with Jesus, and you are one with the Father. Let the impact of Jesus' words saturate your consciousness. These words are revolutionary. They change everything about your identity and they change everything about your relationship with God. You are one with God!

The Circle of Relating

Another important aspect of John 14:16–20 is how it reveals the triune nature of God. In fact, no discussion about answering the question *Who is God?* would be complete without a discussion about the doctrine of the Trinity. The doctrine of the Trinity is not a side point, or just one of many other doctrines. It is a central aspect of the nature of God. Without a revelation of the Trinity, your understanding and therefore your experience with God will be limited.

As you develop your relationship with each member of the Trinity – Father, Son, and Holy Spirit – you will experience greater dimensions of His personality and character. You can know and experience the Holy Spirit as the Spirit of Truth or as the Spirit of Life. You can know and experience Father God as the Father of Lights or the Ancient of Days. And you can know and experience Jesus as Redeemer or King of Kings. I know this may be a bit confusing if you've never really explored the ramifications of the Trinity in scripture, especially in the life of Jesus, but experiencing the fullness of the Godhead is an important part of your union with God in Christ.

In the example I gave earlier with Steve, he experienced Father God as he revisited his memory of being a little boy lying on his bunk bed. However, truthfully and scripturally, Jesus could have been the one to show up in the memory. The Father and Jesus are One, so in reality they were both there. However, if it had been Jesus Steve experienced in his recollection, it probably would have yielded different results. Steve would have possibly received Jesus differently from how he received the Father. Jesus might have felt more like a best friend or a brother. The point is that God showed up as Father to Steve. Why is that?

One of the things I've observed after helping thousands and thousands of people connect with God is that there is usually a primary person of the Trinity they relate to more than the others. A lot of time, when I am speaking at a conference or other event, I'll actually survey the audience. I'll ask people to raise their hands to let me know which member of the Trinity they most naturally relate to. In almost every case, the room will be split into thirds. One-third of the audience will raise their hands indicating they most naturally relate to Father God. Another third will raise their hands signifying they most naturally relate to Jesus. The last third raise their hands saying they feel most connected to Holy Spirit. What is even more interesting is that most people didn't realize they were relating mostly to one member of the Trinity before I asked the question.

Why is this significant? Because, again, it shows how our perceptional filters can influence our relationship with God and limit our view of God without our knowledge. It also points to a huge opportunity to grow and deepen our relationship with God. As the subconscious filters and distortions are removed, our relationship with God grows in ways that were previously unavailable to us. New ways of relating to God as Father, friend, comforter, soul mate, bride, and so forth open up. We are able to receive ministry in areas of our life that we didn't even know needed it. As a result, we experience greater dimensions of God's love and get to know God more intimately.

Why do people tend to connect to one member of the Trinity more than others? And why are they not aware of it? The answer, once again, is found in their past experiences. Our relationships with others tend to subconsciously steer our relationship with God. It makes sense if you really think about it. It seems rather obvious that our relationship with our natural father would influence our ability or desire to relate to Father God. I've seen it go both ways with people who primarily and most naturally relate to God as Father. Some people who prefer Father God had an extremely healthy, loving, and close relationship with their natural father, so relating to God as Father was a no-brainer. Alternatively, others who primarily relate to Father God had distant, absent, or even abusive relationships with their father, so they related best to God as Father out of a subconscious need and desire for a loving father.

The idea that we relate to the Trinity on the basis of our relationships isn't a new concept but is one that is slowly being accepted and recognized. The following table expresses how our natural relationships typically correspond to each member of the Trinity.

Table 1

Member of the Trinity	Provides	Influencers
Father God	Identity Protection Provision Masculinity	Natural Father Male Authority Figures Male Teachers Male Influencers
Holy Spirit	Comfort Nurture Femininity	Natural Mother Female Authority Female Teachers Female Influencers
Jesus	Companionship Friendship Romantic Love	Siblings Friends Boyfriends/Girlfriends Spouses/Ex-Spouses

Source: Adapted from The Father Ladder, Bethel Church Sozo Basic Training (Redding, CA)

How each person subconsciously decides which member of the Trinity they are most comfortable with varies from person to person; however, it is always based on how they bonded with their parents and other key people over the course of their life, especially in childhood. As I said, a person growing up with a very close connection with their natural father might by default most easily relate to God as Father. Conversely, a person who growing up was closest to their mother might most easily relate to Holy Spirit. (Holy Spirit, although depicted as male in scripture, very much embodies the feminine, nurturing attributes of God's personality. If you'll recall, it took both Adam and Eve – male and female – to completely represent the image of God in Genesis.) Similarly, a person who primarily, for whatever reason, bonded deeply with their friends, siblings, or romantic partners and looked to these kinds of relationships to feel loved and accepted might feel most naturally drawn to Jesus.

On the flip side of the coin, there are also scenarios in which people choose the member of the Trinity they are most comfortable with as a strong reaction to what was missing in their childhood or what they learned to avoid throughout. For example, a person who grew up without a mother may gravitate toward Holy Spirit, whereas someone with an abusive mother might find it hard to relate to Holy Spirit. In the end, there isn't a right or wrong answer and it really does differ from person to person. There's no exact science that predicts which way a particular person will go. What's important to know is that everyone has a default preference based on a choice they most likely didn't know they made. People simply decide to relate to a specific member of the Trinity on the basis of a variety of subconscious factors and influences.

The point of all of this is that, as adults, we no longer have to live within these boundaries. We can, with the help of the Holy Spirit, become aware of how we've limited our relationship with God, choose to lay down our limited perceptions of Him, and begin to relate to God in the fullness of who He is.

Experiencing Eternal Life

But, as we wrap up this chapter, I want to tackle one more misconception that can distort your understanding of the gospel and who God is. It's the concept of eternal life. If you grew up in church, you probably memorized John 3:16 in Sunday school:

> *For God so loved the world that he gave his one and only Son, that whoever believes in him shall not perish but have eternal life.*
> – John 3:16 (NIV)

Most people when they hear this scripture think this verse is a message about the afterlife. But eternal life encompasses so much more than that. Eternal life, according to Jesus, isn't just about living forever; it's actually about experiencing a certain kind of life that begins here and now through union with God. In John 17:3, Jesus defines eternal life as having an intimate relationship with God.

And this is eternal life: [it means] to know (to perceive, recognize, become acquainted with, and understand) You, the only true and real God, and [likewise] to know Him, Jesus [as the] Christ (the Anointed One, the Messiah), Whom You have sent.
– John 17:3 (AMPC)

Eternal life means to know and experience you as the only true God, and to know and experience Jesus Christ, as the Son whom you have sent.
– John 17:3 (TPT)

Linking John 3:16 to John 17:3 provides a much clearer picture of the reason Jesus came into the world. It wasn't just so people would go to heaven after they die. Eternal life is something we possess in this life as well. Eternal life is to know and experience God! In the original Greek text, the word translated as *know* is the Greek word *ginosko,* which implies a very intimate and experiential knowing of someone. It's not the kind of knowing you can gain by hearing about them. It's the kind of knowing that you can gain only by personally experiencing them. This is such an important point.

A number of scriptures speak of everlasting life as something we enjoy here and now.

But those who drink the water I give will never be thirsty again. It becomes a fresh, bubbling spring within them, giving them eternal life.
– John 4:14 (NLT)

Very truly I tell you, whoever hears my word and believes Him who sent me has eternal life and will not be judged but has crossed over from death to life.
– John 5:24 (NIV)

Truly, truly, I say to you, whoever believes has eternal life.
– John 6:46 (ESV)

In all of these examples, eternal life is something we have right now. Of course, we will also experience it in heaven after we die, but that's not the point. We don't have to wait. We can know God intimately right here, right now.

In John 10:9, when Jesus said, "I am the door," He wasn't just using colorful language to describe Himself. He is the door to eternal life. We enter into union with God through Jesus and can experience the Father, the Son, and the Holy Spirit from the inside out as a result.

Knowing about God versus Knowing God

In my own life, I didn't learn how to hear God until my 30s. As a result, even though I had grown up in church, I never really knew God. I just knew about Him. It is pretty hard to get to know someone you can't have a conversation with, so everything I knew about God was second-hand. I wasn't experiencing eternal life. I wasn't experiencing my union with God. I didn't even know what that meant.

This is actually one of the biggest problems with religion – it creates a false sense of relationship with God. You think hearing about God means you actually have a relationship with Him. You may go to church every week, read your Bible, memorize scripture, and do all kinds of spiritual things. But that doesn't mean you know God. Unless these activities are helping you experience God intimately, then you are just being religious. Here's what Jesus told the religious leaders in His day:

Here you are scouring through the Scriptures, hoping that you will find eternal life among a pile of scrolls. What you don't seem to understand is that the Scriptures point to Me.
– John 5:39 (Voice)

Interestingly, Jesus rebuked the religious leaders frequently during His ministry. In this case, it was for claiming to know scripture but not recognizing God when He showed up. Even though the Pharisees knew scripture, it didn't mean they actually knew God. It's no coincidence that Jesus didn't choose His disciples from the religious elite of His day. In Acts 4:13; Peter and John are described as ordinary men.

The members of the council were amazed when they saw the boldness of Peter and John, for they could see that they were ordinary men with no special training in the Scriptures. They also recognized them as men who had been with Jesus.
— Acts 4:13 (NLT)

What's interesting to note about this scripture is the description of them "as men who had been with Jesus." It was the disciples' relationship with Jesus that qualified them as ministers, not the amount of scripture they knew. Being with God is what makes us true disciples.

Love Note from Dad

My Magnificent Child,

My heart longs for you to experience Me as I really am. Second-hand knowledge of your Father is never ideal. Now is the time to release the misconceptions that have painted a distorted picture of Me in your heart. I am not like any other person you have ever met. No, there is none like Me. My perfect love is one of a kind.

You can never exhaust My patience. I never lose My temper or speak to you harshly. You do not get in trouble with Me when you do something wrong. Nothing can change My opinion of you. But the pain you've experienced in your human relationships has a way of hindering our relationship. The rejection, betrayal, and disappointment you've experienced with people cause you to fear intimacy.

Pain left to run its course will always cause your heart to harden and become calloused. But in its attempt to protect you, it actually desensitizes you, and hinders your ability to feel My love. As you sit in My presence, and marinate in My Spirit, your heart will become tender once again. I am not just a pain reliever, I am a pain remover. I will take away your pain and make your heart new. Come into the light of My love, precious one. With Me there is nothing to fear. The light of My love will erase the pain of your past and set your heart ablaze with My passion for you.

There's no one else on the planet who knows you the way I do. I know the number of hairs on your head. I know your thoughts before you think them and your words before you speak them. I live inside of you, child. I feel your emotions and experience all that you go through from your perspective as well as Mine.

But it's not enough that I know you this way. I want you to know Me this way. My union with you in Christ gives you access to My thoughts and My emotions. I want you to experience the way I think and the way I feel about you, about what's important to you, about everything. I promise you are going to be surprised by My heart. I am not like most people think I am. There's not a religious bone in my body. I am relational, not religious. My vision is for the church to be my family, not an institution. My kingdom is full of My kids, not My subjects.

But, really, the best way for you to get to know Me is to experience Me yourself. Trust isn't built on words but on actions. You need to experience My love in action. You need to experience My faithfulness yourself. That's the way any good relationship is developed. Spending time together is the only way you'll really get to know Me for who I really am.

Kisses from Heaven,
Dad

Digging Deeper Exercise – Writing Your God Story

In this exercise, we will be uncovering and unpacking the experiences in your life that shaped your image of God and negatively impacted whom you believe Him to be. We will also be taking some time to forgive and release those who negatively influenced your relationship with God. The goal is to invite God to reshape your image of Him so that you can get to know Him for who He really is.

STEP 1 – Scripture Reading

Begin by reading Matthew 16:13–20 (NIV).

> *When Jesus came to the region of Caesarea Philippi, he asked his disciples, "Who do people say the Son of Man is?" They replied, "Some say John the Baptist; others say Elijah; and still others, Jeremiah or one of the prophets." "But what about you?" he asked. "Who do you say I am?" Simon Peter answered, "You are the Messiah, the Son of the living God." Jesus replied, "Blessed are you, Simon son of Jonah, for this was not revealed to you by flesh and blood, but by my Father in heaven. And I tell you that you are Peter, and on this rock I will build my church, and the gates of Hades will not overcome it. I will give you the keys of the kingdom of heaven; whatever you bind on earth will be bound in heaven, and whatever you loose on earth will be loosed in heaven." Then he ordered his disciples not to tell anyone that he was the Messiah.*
> *– Matthew 16:13-20 (NIV)*

As you can see from this scripture, in Jesus' day, people were very confused about who he was. But Peter, when he identified Jesus as the Son of God, was told that he didn't get his opinion from other people but from the Father Himself.

The goal of this exercise is to begin to sift through who we believe God is based on the opinions of others. This would include our family of origin, our church background or lack thereof, the media, popular opinion, and so forth.

STEP 2 - Journal Your History with God

In your journal, reflect and write about your life history with God. Think of it as writing your "God story." Include your earliest memories about God or with God. Include the process of being introduced to God and the process of desiring a relationship with Him. Travel through the various life experiences that you've had with others who represented God to you, including family members, spiritual leaders, church experiences, youth camps, or any other experiences that shaped your current relationship with God. Make sure that you include both positive and negative experiences. Include the high points and low points of your spiritual journey and make sure you identify things that could be considered defining moments in your relationship with God.

If you are a new believer or haven't yet really settled on what you believe about God, then just describe your process or even lack of process in getting where you are today. Don't overthink it – just write as though you were talking to your best friend. Also, if you'd rather not write it down, then record your story on your phone. Afterward, you can transcribe it. The key is to write or speak freely.

As you document your history with God, think about the following questions and write down your answers in your journal. Invite God into your thoughts and allow the Holy Spirit to bring up past situations and memories. The goal is to identify how religion has negatively impacted your relationship with God so that you can release these things and give God a clean slate.

- Growing up, what did your parents, grandparents, aunts and uncles, and other significant family members believe about God?
- Does any one family member or do a couple of family members stand out as key influencers in your life as it relates to God?
- If so, why? What specifically did you learn from them?
- Are there specific memories or experiences that you can remember that dramatically shaped your view of God the Father and how He sees you?
- Are there specific memories or experiences that you can remember that dramatically shaped your view of Jesus and how He sees you?
- Are there specific memories or experiences that you can remember that dramatically shaped your view of the Holy Spirit?

- Are there specific memories or experiences that you can remember that dramatically shaped your view of the church?
- Are there specific memories or experiences that you can remember that dramatically shaped your view of Christians?
- What was your salvation experience like?
- What other people come to mind as having an influence on your image of God? This would include teachers, church leaders, authors, etc. How did they influence you?
- What spiritual experiences, either positive or negative, have influenced your image of God?
- What are the things that have happened in your life or the things you have observed that have hindered your ability to believe that God is Love?
- What are the things that have happened in your life or the things you have observed that have hindered your ability to believe that God is good?
- What are the things that have happened in your life or the things you have observed that have hindered your ability to believe that God is who He says He is?

STEP 3 - Identify Defining Moments

Once your God story is written, read your story out loud to yourself. If you remember other events or want to add or edit something, go ahead. Take some time to finalize what you've written. The length of the story isn't what's important; it's more about identifying moments and things that shaped and defined your relationship with God. After you finalize your story, go back and highlight key words and phrases that jump out at you. Notice how your relationship with God was impacted by religion. Are there specific experiences that connected or disconnected you to God? Try to pinpoint which specific experiences – both positive and negative – were defining moments for you in your relationship with God. These are the times you felt most connected and disconnected from God.

If you can, identity at least the most positive and negative experiences. Be specific. The experiences that come to mind quickly are best. Don't overthink it. Focus on the highest highs and the lowest lows.

Summarize each defining moment or experience with God as follows:

- What was your approximate age at the time of the experience?
- Summarize the experience in a couple of sentences.
- What did you believe about God as a result of the experience?

STEP 4 - Forgive Influencers

In this step, we are going to take a very important step toward connecting with God as Father, Son, and Holy Spirit in a deeper and more meaningful way by forgiving the people who were key influencers or authority figures in our lives who fell short of representing God's perfect love to us and negatively impacted our image of God.

It is important to remember, especially when forgiving people who hurt us deeply, that forgiving someone is not the same thing as saying what happened is okay. Forgiveness also doesn't mean that you have to let the person back into your inner circle or even be in a relationship with them.

Forgiveness is always about you. It's about you releasing the pain of what happened so that you feel at peace. Reconciliation after forgiveness is an entirely different matter. That is something that may or may not happen depending on the other person's ability to be in a healthy relationship with you.

As we pray the following prayer of forgiveness and release the key influencers and authority figures who were present in your childhood, keep in mind, we are not dishonoring anyone in any way but rather simply acknowledging that they were an imperfect representation of a perfect God. We are forgiving them for whatever ways they misrepresented God's love.

This includes ways they may have interacted and related with you that were not how God interacts and relates to you. It also includes things that they should have done to accurately represent God's love but didn't or didn't know how to do. Really, we are forgiving them for anything that negatively impacted your image of God or that has hindered your ability to relate to Him as He really is – good, perfect, and full of joy!

When you are ready, begin by praying the following prayer out loud for every key influencer in your life. Refer back to Table 1 often and ask the Holy Spirit to bring to remembrance everyone that you need to forgive.

Father God, Holy Spirit, and Jesus, I choose by an act of my will to forgive
_____ *(insert the name of the person you are forgiving) for being an imperfect representation of You and for negatively influencing my image of You.*

- *For acting in ways that were not like You*
- *For saying things that were not from You*
- *And for treating me in ways that were not like You*

I also forgive _____ *(name) for not doing and saying the things they should have, things that would have painted a more accurate image of who You are on my heart.*

Specifically, I forgive them for _____
_____ *(list anything and everything that comes to mind). I release these things to You, Lord, along with the hurt and pain and* _____ *(other emotions) they caused. I release them and let them go.*

In Jesus' name, I renounce the lies that were planted in my heart as a result of these things and give You permission to replace them with the truth of who You are. I ask You to smash my distorted image of You _____ *(Father, Holy Spirit, or Jesus) that was built as a result of their imperfections.*

Tear down every wall that has kept me from experiencing You. Reveal Yourself to me in spirit and in truth. Show me who You are and how much I am loved. Take back the ground in my life that the enemy has stolen as a result of these things. In Jesus' name I pray, AMEN!

STEP 5 – Remove Perceptional Filters

The goal in this step is to identify and remove the filters and distorted lenses that you've been viewing God through. Remember, while we may think of ourselves as open-minded and objective about God, our relationship with Him and our ability to relate to Him as Father, friend, and soul mate is greatly influenced by the beliefs, paradigms, notions, and ideas that we learned and inherited from our family of origin, upbringing, church background, experiences with Christians and the supernatural, as well as other life experiences.

In this step, the goal is to expose these things for what they are – lies – and replace them with the truth, biblically and experientially, so that a new foundation for relating to God can be laid.

STEP 6 – Prayer to Remove Lenses

Begin by praying the following prayer out loud:

Father in Heaven, Grant unto me the Spirit of wisdom and understanding in the knowledge of You. Help me identify the filters and lenses that have distorted my image of You. Show me the lenses (i.e., glasses) that I have been viewing You through that have hindered my ability to see You clearly. (Write down what you see in your journal.)

Tear down every wall and uproot every lie. Renew my mind and lead and guide me into the truth. Enlighten my eyes, open my ears, take me where I need to go to unpack and release the things that are keeping me from experiencing You as You really are.

By faith, I renounce every filter that has distorted my image of You and remove the lenses that have hindered my ability to see You clearly. Jesus, I now hand these lenses to You along with judgments that I have made about You, our Father, and the Holy Spirit. Restore my sight so that I can see you clearly.

(Place your hands over your eyes and symbolically remove the glasses. Hand them to Jesus and then ask Him what He wants to give you in return.)

Jesus, what do You have to give me in return? (Using your spiritual eyes, see what Jesus hands you.)

What do you want to tell me about this gift? (Engage as many of your spiritual senses as appropriate – seeing, hearing, smelling, tasting, and touching. Write down what you experience in your journal.)

Holy Spirit, thank you for enlightening the eyes of my understanding and helping me see You clearly from this day forward. Cleanse my conscience from dead works. Cause me to rise above the things that I have learned, wrongly believed, and experienced. Show me how to sit with You in the heavenly places and see things from Your perspective.

Help me experience the reality of the Father's perfect love as I experience my union with You. Help me to experience the comfort, grace, and joy of the Holy Spirit that lives in me. Help me to step into the reality of the kingdom within.

In Jesus' name, AMEN!

STEP 7 - Write a Letter to the Godhead

On a new page in your journal, write a letter/prayer to the Godhead (Father, Son, and Holy Spirit) expressing your desire for more revelation of the Trinity. Speak to each member of the Trinity individually. Ask the Holy Spirit to enlighten your eyes and give you imaginations of the Father, Jesus, and the Holy Spirit as you write.

When you are ready to go deeper, go through the following exercises step by step, asking the Holy Spirit to lead and guide you into all truth.

- Ask Holy Spirit to show you a lie that you currently believe about the Father based on your upbringing.
- Ask Him why you believe this lie and when you started believing the lie.
- Ask Him if there is someone you need to forgive for teaching you this lie. If so, pray the prayer of forgiveness in step 4.
- Ask Him to show you the truth, and engage your spiritual senses to receive the truth.
- Write down everything the Lord shows you in your journal.

Repeat steps 1–6 with Jesus and the Holy Spirit.

CHAPTER FIVE

The 2nd Big Q: Who Am I?

Who in the world am I? Ah, that's the great puzzle.
– Lewis Carroll, *Alice in Wonderland*

I had this fake ID in college, before I was of legal drinking age, that I used to gain access to bars and night clubs. Honestly, it was the worst fake ID ever. I didn't look anything like the picture. But surprisingly it worked; no one ever questioned if it was me or not. They apparently thought it *was* me. Sadly, the fact of the matter is that a lot of people are unknowingly walking around carrying a fake ID. Their self-image doesn't look anything like the person God created them to be. If they ever saw themselves through God's eyes, they wouldn't recognize themselves. As a result, they go through life impersonating someone they're not. But no one, including themselves, can tell the difference.

Without an intimate relationship with God, it's impossible to know who you really are. God is the author of your identity and only He can define you. Time and time again in scripture, God revealed people's true identities to them. Up until that point, they thought of themselves completely different from how God did. Joseph was just his father's favorite son, who wore a coat of many colors, before God gave him a dream (Genesis 37:1–10). Moses, for example, didn't see himself as this great deliverer of the nation of Israel (Exodus 3:1–17).

He was just a shepherd tending his flock before his encounter with God at the burning bush. David was just a shepherd boy, before Samuel anointed him to be king (1 Samuel 16:1–13). Simon was a fisherman, before Jesus changed His name to Peter and called him a rock (Matthew 16:17–18).

Your true identity is God-given. Only He can reveal what He had in mind when He created you. This is why most people, at some level, struggle in their relationship with themselves and to develop healthy self-esteem. Without an experiential relationship with God, you will always be carrying around a fake ID. You will, to some extent, feel uncomfortable in your own skin and struggle to find a sense of yourself. You were created in God's image by God Himself. But even more than that, you've been re-created in Christ (Ephesians 2:10 AMP). Your true identity, therefore, can only be found in relationship to Jesus. When God thought of you before the foundation of the world, he planned for you to be a part of the Triune family – Father, Son, and Holy Spirit – by placing you *in Christ*.

> *Even before he made the world, God loved us and chose us in Christ to be holy and without fault in his eyes. God decided in advance to adopt us into his own family by bringing us to himself through Jesus Christ. This is what He wanted to do, and it gave Him great pleasure.*
> – Ephesians 1:4–5 (NLT)

Your True Identity

Your re-created identity in Christ is your *true identity*. This is why it must be unveiled within the context of your relationship with God. Your true identity is invisible to the naked eye because it is *spiritual in nature*. The same was true for Jesus. Jesus' identity wasn't based on some earthly, physical reality. He wasn't defined by his earthly parents, his occupation as a carpenter, or people's opinions of Him. He was defined by His relationship with His Heavenly Father.

> *While He was still speaking, a bright cloud covered them, and a voice from the cloud said, "This is my Son, whom I love; with Him I am well pleased. Listen to Him!"*
> – Matthew 17:5 (NIV)

Jesus didn't allow anyone's opinion to shape his self-concept even though the people of His day had all kinds of opinions about Him. In Matthew 16, when Jesus asks His disciples the question, "Who do men say that I am?" Their answers were quite surprising.

He asked His disciples, "Who do people say that the Son of Man is?" His disciples replied, "Well," they replied, "some say John the Baptist, some say Elijah, and others say Jeremiah or one of the prophets."
– Matthew 16:13–14 (NLT)

This is a perfect example of how the perception of others can get wrapped up in your identity. But other people's opinions are no way to define yourself. People think all kinds of crazy things. In Jesus' case, they thought he was a reincarnation of a bunch of dead people. This just goes to show you how insane other people's opinions about you can be. These folks were totally off base. They had no idea who Jesus really was. Thankfully, Jesus wasn't confused. He got His identity solely from the Father. He was the beloved Son who gave the Father great joy.

As Jesus continued His conversation with His disciples, He was basically saying, "Okay, that's what other people are saying, but what about you guys? Who do you say I am?" Simon Peter steps up and speaks in agreement with who Jesus actually was. Under the inspiration of the Holy Spirit, he nailed it. Jesus was the Messiah, the Son of God.

Then he asked them, "But who do you say I am?" Simon Peter answered, "You are the Messiah, the Son of the living God." Jesus replied, "You are blessed, Simon son of John, because my Father in heaven has revealed this to you. You did not learn this from any human being. Now I say to you that you are Peter (which means 'rock'), and upon this rock I will build my church, and all the powers of hell will not conquer it."
– Matthew 16:15–18 (NLT)

Jesus' response to Peter's revelation was a pivotal turning point in Peter's life. Before this moment, Peter's name had been Simon. His whole life, Peter had been carrying around a fake ID of some guy named Simon. In the Greek,

Simon means "reed." But Peter, right after he revealed Jesus' true identity, got his real ID. He wasn't a reed. He was a rock. In that moment, something miraculous happened. Peter saw himself for the very first time from the Father's perspective.

In the same way the Father had revealed who Jesus was to Peter, the Father was now revealing who Peter was to Peter. In an instant Peter discovered the answer to the question, *Who am I?* Peter went from being an unstable reed that sways in the wind every time a little breeze blows to an impenetrable rock. Reeds are flimsy. You can't build anything on a reed – that's just silly. But a rock? You can build something solid on a foundation made of rock.

The Identity Cycle

As awesome as it was for Peter to have a new name that meant rock, what was happening in that moment wasn't just for Peter, it was also applicable to you and me. When Jesus told Peter He was going to build His church upon *this rock,* Jesus was speaking both literally and metaphorically. Yes, Jesus was going to use Peter's life as a foundational part of building His church. But it was much more than that. In scripture, Jesus is the described as *The Rock.*

> *The stone which the builders rejected has become the chief corner stone.*
> – Psalms 118:22 (NASB)

> *And all drank the same spiritual drink, for they were drinking from*
> *a spiritual rock which followed them; and the rock was Christ.*
> – 1 Corinthians 10:4 (NASB)

> *And coming to Him as to a living stone which has been rejected by men, but is*
> *choice and precious in the sight of God.*
> – 1 Peter 2:4 (NASB)

If Jesus is *The Rock,* what was He actually saying to Peter? Why did Simon need to ditch his fake ID and change his name? Simon was renamed Peter, or rock, because, from the Father's perspective, Simon's true identity was found in Christ, who is *The Rock.* Peter, a rock, was in Jesus Christ, *The Rock.* Ultimately, Jesus changing Peter's name was about much more than Peter. It was a prophetic picture of the church – the new creation *in Christ*. I know this may be a little difficult to wrap your head around, but from the Father's perspective, our true identity is always wrapped up in Christ. That is why the church is called the body of Christ. It's a picture of oneness. Jesus is the head and we are His body.

> *Now you are the body of Christ and individually members of it.*
> – 1 Corinthians 12:27 (ESV)

> *And He is the head of the body, the church. He is the beginning, the firstborn from the dead, that in everything He might be preeminent.*
> – Colossians 1:18 (ESV)

The way Peter discovered his true identity is the way all of us discover our true identity. I call it the Identity Cycle. If you want to know who you are, you must first realize who Jesus is. Why? Because your true identity is found *in Him*. Your identification with Christ is the foundation of your true identity. This is what it means to be *in Christ*. Like Peter, we too are called rock, because we've been placed in Christ Jesus, who is The Rock.

You Are Not Just Human

Without a revelation of Christ in you, it's impossible to form an accurate self-image. Without an accurate self-image, it's impossible for you to receive God's purpose for your life. The reason is that your purpose is supernatural. It's not something you would ever be able to accomplish in your humanity. It requires that you operate as a child of God, who lives in union with the Father, the way Jesus did. When Jesus declared that the Father and I are one, this statement not only revealed His identity, it revealed how He was able to fulfill His divine destiny. The same is true for you and me. This is why you must understand you are in Christ as you answer the question, Who am I? Any answer you may come up with that isn't firmly rooted in your union with God will fall terribly short of defining who you really are. It will also cause you to underestimate your life purpose.

The simple but powerful revelation of "Christ in you/you in Christ" changes everything about your self-perception. I know, because I've experienced it personally and I'm seeing it happen to Emergers every day. When you realize you are one with God in Christ, you go from being a powerless person to someone who sees miracles on a daily basis. You go from never hearing God to realizing you have 24/7 access to God's thoughts and an ability to hear from Him all the time.

Unfortunately, the illusion of separation from God has been so ingrained in us that, for the most part, we operate totally unaware of God's indwelling presence. Sure, we've been taught Bible stories. But what about learning how our union with God causes our lives to look like a Bible story? Most believers have listened to tons of teaching on topics like prayer and Bible study and have spent countless days pursuing spiritual disciplines. But how much time have we spent learning how to abide in Christ?

As a result of this imbalance, we've ended up with a really distorted works-oriented view of the gospel and a very distorted image of ourselves. By default, without even really thinking about it, we tend to view and perceive God somewhere "out there" or "up there," definitely outside of ourselves.

Jesus in a Schlyce Suit

In my own life, when God was attempting to reshape my self-image, He asked me to meditate on a single scripture for an entire year. The scripture was from Colossians 1:27.

To them God willed to make known what are the riches of the glory of this mystery among the Gentiles: which is Christ in you, the hope of glory.
– Colossians 1:27 (NKJV)

Before this assignment from the Lord, it never occurred to me to spend an extended time meditating on one scripture. I thought you were supposed to follow a daily Bible reading plan or read the Bible through in a year. But after the incredible transformation that occurred in my own life after sticking with Colossians 1:27 for a year, I recognize that it's the quality, not the quantity, of scripture you know. Just because you have memorized a scripture and can recite it like a parrot doesn't mean you've been transformed by it. And, frankly, until you have been transformed by a revelation of your union with God, you will remain clueless about who you really are.

It wasn't long after I started meditating on the idea of "Christ in me" that I heard the Holy Spirit tell me to go and stand in front of the mirror. He told me to look at myself, to stare at myself, until I could see Jesus in me. At first, all I saw was my own reflection. It reminded me of myself all those years ago as a child when I would stand in front of the mirror rhetorically asking myself, "Who am I?" God definitely has a sense of humor. Here I was, over two decades later, doing the same thing. But this time, my world was about to be rocked.

As I stood there staring at my own reflection, the Holy Spirit said, "Use your spiritual eyes, Schlyce. You are 'Jesus wearing a Schlyce suit.'" Instantly, I had an inspired imagination. I saw Jesus "wearing" me like He would wear a Halloween costume. My face completely covered His face. He was wearing a Schlyce mask. But you couldn't tell it was a mask. It looked exactly like me. I was dumbfounded, and the Holy Spirit continued to speak to me. He said, "That's great, Schlyce, but you aren't really getting it. When you think of Jesus, you think of the nice man who strolled along the sea of Galilee with His disciples. That's not the Jesus that is living in you. If you want to meet the Jesus that is inside of you, read Revelation chapter one."

I, John, who also am your brother, and companion in tribulation, and in the kingdom and patience of Jesus Christ, was in the isle that is called Patmos, for the word of God, and for the testimony of Jesus Christ. I was in the Spirit on the Lord's day, and heard behind me a great voice, as of a trumpet, Saying, I am Alpha and Omega, the first and the last: and, What thou seest, write in a book, and send it unto the seven churches which are in Asia; unto Ephesus, and unto Smyrna, and unto Pergamos, and unto Thyatira, and unto Sardis, and unto Philadelphia, and unto Laodicea. And I turned to see the voice that spake with me. And being turned, I saw seven golden candlesticks; And in the midst of the seven candlesticks one like unto the Son of Man, clothed with a garment down to the foot, and girt about the paps with a golden girdle. His head and his hairs were white like wool, as white as snow; and his eyes were as a flame of fire; And his feet like unto fine brass, as if they burned in a furnace; and his voice as the sound of many waters. And he had in his right hand seven stars: and out of his mouth went a sharp two-edged sword: and his countenance was as the sun shineth in his strength.

*And when I saw him, I fell at his feet as dead. And he laid his right hand upon me,
saying unto me, Fear not; I am the first and the last: I am he that liveth, and was dead;
and, behold, I am alive for evermore, Amen; and have the keys of hell and of death.*
— Revelation 1:9–18 (KJV)

As I read these words, a light bulb went off inside of me. There's a huge difference between the Jesus who died on the cross and the Jesus who came out of the grave. The Jesus described in Revelation 1 is the resurrected Lord Jesus. This Jesus has white hair and eyes that burn like flames of fire. His voice thunders like the waves and his face shines as bright as the sun. He has the keys of hell and of death. All I could think was, "Holy cow, this is who lives in me?" It was then that I heard the Holy Spirit tell me to look in the mirror again, except this time to look into my eyes. He said to stand there until I could see Jesus' eyes of fire inside of mine.

Then I saw it. I still remember it vividly; my face began to morph into Jesus' and then back into mine. It reminded me of how in the movies, they use special effects to morph an ordinary person into a super-hero or something. I could see the flames in his eyes burning inside of mine. I wasn't really morphing into Jesus – I was still standing in my bathroom looking in the mirror – but it felt very real. After a few minutes, my reflection returned to normal. It was just me staring at myself in the mirror. But I was different. I couldn't take my eyes off of my eyes. Using my spiritual eyes, I could still see the fire burning within them. Jesus *really was* living inside of me.

The Supernatural Is Normal

After that day, incredible things started to happen in my life. Without knowing what I was doing, the Holy Spirit would lead me to talk to random people on the street. The first time it happened, I was living in downtown Chicago. I was on the way to work and made my usual stop at Starbucks to grab a latte. As I walked into Starbucks, I noticed a homeless lady sitting outside. I didn't think that much of it. As I waited for my coffee, however, I heard the Holy Spirit say, "Go outside and talk to that lady." I remember looking around thinking, "Who me?" But then I heard the Holy Spirit say, "Yes, you. Go outside and talk to that lady." I'd never done anything like that before. I was the furthest thing from an evangelist you could think of. But I couldn't shake the Holy Spirit. I could feel His presence pressing down on me. I was super-uncomfortable with the idea and started arguing with Him in my head. "Who am I to talk to that Lady? I don't know what to say. I'm late to work." I came up with every excuse in the book. But the Holy Spirit was persistent. He wouldn't let it go.

To make a long story short, I ended up talking to the lady. Her name was Alice. She was a drug addict who lived on the streets. She had been praying to God for freedom. She was trained as a nurse and had kids at home, but she was hopelessly addicted to drugs. Crack was her drug of choice and she wasn't able to kick her daily habit. I ended up taking her to my church that following Sunday. She was so high when I picked her up, I was totally freaked out. But she somehow stumbled down to the altar and gave her life to Jesus.

She was baptized that same day and when she came out of the water, the power of God hit her. She was stone-cold sober. She was completely delivered of her addiction in an instant. We ended up going to lunch afterward and having a lovely conversation. After that, Alice began to introduce me to her other drug addict friends. I ended up ministering, even though I wasn't a "minister," to all of them. Miracle after miracle started happening in some of the roughest neighborhoods in Chicago. Even though I didn't know what I was doing, I did know who I was. I was Jesus wearing a Schlyce suit. My eyes were on fire just like His.

The revelation of Christ in me was so powerful that there were many times when my very presence would cause evil spirits to manifest. It was like I was living a Bible story. I remember one time being in this drug house and everyone there started to go into a seizure all at once. Normally, I would have called 911, but instead, by the power of the Holy Spirit, everyone was set free. Another time, I was just sitting in my car, and this guy came up and knocked on my window. At first, I was frightened, but when I rolled down my window, I just put my hand on his head and he was totally delivered from heroin addiction. I could write several books about the supernatural, miraculous things that began to happen in my life that year as I meditated on Colossians 1:27. I saw deaf people totally healed and metal rods in people's backs dissolve. I saw all kinds of diseases healed and encountered so many deliverances, I lost count. The very same things you read about Jesus doing in His earthly ministry, He was doing through me. It was a crazy adventure for sure.

Very truly I tell you, whoever believes in me will do the works I have been doing,
and they will do even greater things than these, because I am going to the Father.
– John 14:12 (NIV)

Schlyce in a Jesus Suit

As if that year's scripture meditation project wasn't exciting enough, I had no idea that I was about to find out there was more to the story than what I was already experiencing. Jesus was just getting warmed up. The next year, I received another meditation project. Once again, I was to concentrate on one scripture for the whole year. This time, the scripture was Ephesians 2:6.

For he raised us from the dead along with Christ and seated us with him in the
heavenly realms because we are united with Christ Jesus.
– Ephesians 2:6 (NLT)

The meditation kicked off with a bang. The revelation of my union with God through Jesus was exploding in my heart. Except this time, the perspective was "me in Christ" instead of "Christ in me." Instead of Jesus wearing a Schlyce suit, I was wearing a Jesus suit. My life was literally hidden in Christ (Colossians 3:3). My identification with Christ was becoming solidified in my heart. The gospel became a union with God message to me. I finally understood what the Apostle Paul was trying to say all throughout his epistles. I was to fully identify with Jesus. I was crucified with Jesus (Galatians 2:2). I was buried with Jesus (Romans 6:3–4). I was raised with Jesus (Colossians 3:1). I had ascended to the right hand of God with Jesus (Ephesians 2:6). Even though I was born two thousand years after Jesus, I was mystically united with Him in His death, burial, resurrection, and ascension. And now, my life was hidden inside of Him.

In the same way, Jesus could say the Father and He were one. I could now say the same thing. My union with Jesus, who was one with the Father, was also my union with the Father. But even more powerful than that, if that's even possible, was what happened to my previous identity. It ceased to exist. The "me" that existed apart from Jesus died with Jesus on the cross. I was a new creation living in perpetual union with God Almighty. The only "me" that existed was the "me" sandwiched in the middle of Christ. That's why I like to describe our perpetual union with God as the Jesus Sandwich. I must warn you though, if you're going to fully enjoy your Jesus Sandwich, you are going to need to let go of a lot of things you may have believed about yourself. Some of which you probably learned in church! Trust me, bad doctrine will ruin your appetite.

Solving the Identity Crisis

The New Testament has an enormous amount to say about who we are as new creations in Christ. One of the biggest misconceptions is that you, as a believer, still have a sin nature. While this might seem like a bold statement, it is a biblical one. The New Testament is clear. Jesus dealt a death blow to sin once and for all on the cross. Jesus didn't just forgive sins, he became sin (2 Corinthians 5:21). In Christ, you are no longer a sinner, you are a saint (Romans 6:2–11, 1 Corinthians 1:2). Your old sinful self has been crucified (Galatians 2:20). You are free (Galatians 5:1). You are righteous (2 Corinthians 5:21). You are perfect (Hebrews 10:14). And you are blameless (Ephesians 1:4). This is why there's no condemnation (Romans 8:1). Your sin nature was crucified on Christ's cross.

I realize this may be news to a large percentage of the Christian population. Many wrongly support the idea that believers have two natures – a sin nature and God's righteous nature. But that makes no sense. You can't be righteous and unrighteous at the same time. Either you are righteous or you are not. It is like being pregnant. Either you are or you are not. You cannot be just a little pregnant. In the same way, you cannot be in Christ and be separated from Him at the same time. In Christ, as opposed to the Old Covenant, your righteousness is not based on your good behavior or performance, it's based on you being in Christ. In Christ, you are just like Jesus.

This is how love is made complete among us so that we will have confidence on the day of judgment: In this world we are like Jesus.
– 1 John 4:17 (NIV)

I know what you're probably thinking right about now. Something along the lines of "If there's no sin problem anymore, why do we sin?" That's a very good question. One that is pivotal in your relationship with yourself and with God. People sin simply because they don't know how not to, *yet*. You aren't struggling with a sin nature, you are struggling with a sin habit. Most people just have never been told they don't have a sin nature. So, they believe they are still sinners. Which, if that is what you believe about yourself, how do you think you are going to act? Like a sinner, of course. It's simply Proverbs 23:7, "As he thinks in his heart, so is he," in action.

You see, our ongoing problem with sin is not really about our behavior at all. It's about us carrying around a fake ID. The way we act, yes, even sin, is the result of an identity crisis. Sin is the symptom of not knowing who you are in Christ. The solution isn't to focus on sin, it is to focus on who you really are. It's a mind renewal issue, not a human nature one.

Awake to righteousness, and sin not."
– 1 Corinthians 15:34 (NJKV)

As this powerful scripture states, when you awake to righteousness your behavior will automatically change. In other words, if your mind is renewed to who you are in Christ, you will act like Christ. Sin is the fruit of an unrighteous self-image. Fortunately or unfortunately, your perception of what is true about you is ruling you. When your self-concept is aligned with who you are in Christ, you will live out of your true identity. But, to whatever extent your self-concept has aligned with your fake ID, you will live out of a false identity.

Even though there are tons of scriptures that describe who you are in Christ, until you really grasp it for yourself, you will still be running around with a fake ID. You will continue living with a false persona, believing your identity is based on who you perceive yourself to be. The challenge is this: We can read about who the Bible says we are until we are blue in the face, but we need to experience it! Of course, this is why I wrote this book and developed Emerge. It is time for you to cut up that fake ID and experience who you are in Christ. As you read this chapter's love letter from God and work through the Digging Deeper Exercise, expect something to shift in your heart. The Father is about to reveal who you really are and help you answer the question "Who am I?" once and for all.

Love Letter from God

My Powerful Child,

Gaze deep into My eyes and tell me what you see. If you look long enough, you will see yourself, hidden inside of Me. When I look in the mirror, it's not just My reflection that makes Me smile. You live and move and have your being in Me, My love. Seeing you in Me is what delights My heart.

Oh how I long for you to see yourself as you really are – wrapped up in Christ, perfect and complete. Life has taught you many things about yourself that simply are not true. But, now is the time to hear who you really are, and let Me redefine you. Melt into Me, child, and experience what is real. Tune your ear to My thoughts. Focus so that you can see what I see. I promise you will be amazed by the glory that is hidden inside of you.

Look closely, child, and agree with how you look from My perspective. You are clothed with My majesty, crowned with My honor, and full of My power. You are dressed in My righteousness, washed in My blood, and shining bright as the sun. You couldn't be more perfect or loved than you are right in this very moment. You are altogether lovely to Me.

You are my beloved child, in whom I am well pleased. There's nothing in all of creation that can separate or come between us. Settle into My perfect love, child. Make your home inside of Me. This is the place Jesus prepared for you. In Me is where you belong.

Kisses from Heaven,
Dad

Digging Deeper Exercise - Destroying Your Fake ID

In this Digging Deeper Exercise, you are going to be partnering with the Holy Spirit to transform your self-image. You'll be using your spiritual senses to visualize your union with God through Christ and speaking scriptures over yourself in the form of "I am" statements. The outward expression of the new creation, the reality of Christ within, is produced in our lives only to the extent that we renew our minds (Romans 12:2). It's not the truth we hear that sets us free, but the truth we come to know experientially (Greek *gnosko*).

STEP 1 - Mirror Work

Standing in front of the mirror visualizing who you are and speaking your true identity over yourself is a simple, yet powerful, way to experience transformation. I encourage you to continue these exercises on a daily basis as long as needed until you are established in the reality of who you are in Christ. As you recite, meditate, and visualize on the scriptural truths in this exercise, you will find yourself moving beyond intellectual knowledge into truly knowing and experiencing the truth that sets you free.

Naturally speaking, transformation is not as simple as one would hope. That's because our beliefs, referred to as strongholds in the Bible, are held mostly subconsciously. Every human being on the planet has strongholds or areas of their minds that need to be renewed (Romans 12:2). Really, any area of our lives where our thinking is not in agreement (at a subconscious level) with the mind of Christ needs to be renewed.

Our currently held beliefs or strongholds were formed over the course of our lifetime through the various life experiences we experienced. Replacing wrong beliefs, called unbelief in the Bible, requires that we not just mentally agree with truth but also re-experience what we believe to be truth for ourselves. These experiences can be real or imagined; our minds don't know the difference. Throughout scripture, meditation is positioned as a primary way to experience the truth of God's word and transform what we believe (Joshua 1:8; Psalm 1:2, 4:4, 23:7, 63:6, 143:55; Philippians 4:8).

STEP 2 – Visualizing Your Union with Christ

Set aside at least 20 minutes for this exercise at a time you can be alone without interruptions or distractions. Stand in front of a full-length mirror if you have one; if not, a bathroom mirror will also work. Before you begin, pray the following prayer aloud:

Holy Spirit, Today as I stand in front of the mirror, enlighten my eyes, open my ears, and activate my spiritual senses of touch, taste, and smell. Make the spiritual realm real to me. I yield my imagination, my thoughts, and my body to You as an instrument of righteousness. I offer myself as a living sacrifice. Reveal the truth to me. Supernaturally renew my mind. Change my self-concept and help me experience the real me. Empower me to see myself as I really am. Show me what it means to live in union with Jesus. I give you permission to transform my identity and bring my self-image into alignment with who I am in Christ. In Jesus' name, AMEN!

As you stand in front of the mirror staring at your reflection:

- Imagine Christ in you (Colossians 1:27).
- Imagine Jesus wearing you like a suit. He is wearing your skin, seeing through your eyes, thinking through your mind, and infusing your spirit.
- You might find the room you are in transforming into another place. If this happens, go with the flow and allow Jesus to show you whatever He wants.
- After about 10 minutes, change your perspective.
- Now imagine you being in Christ (Ephesians 2:6).
- Imagine yourself wearing Jesus like a suit. Imagine you are wearing Jesus' skin, seeing through His eyes, thinking through His mind, your spirits intertwined as one.
- Again, you might find the room transforming into another place. If this happens, once again, just go with the flow and allow Jesus to show you whatever He wants.
- Make sure to jot down whatever revelations or encounters you are experiencing in your journal.

STEP 3 – Speaking "I Am"

As you stand in front of the mirror, read each of the following scriptural "I am" statements over yourself out loud. Make the statement a declaration of what is true. As you speak, look and listen with your spiritual eyes and ears to see and hear what the Holy Spirit may be revealing to you. Pause as needed. Revelation and encounters are the goal. Let the Spirit show you "you!"

- I am a partaker of God's divine nature (2 Peter 1:3–4).
- I am the temple of the Holy Spirit (1 Corinthians 6:19).
- I am one with Jesus and have the mind of Christ (1 Corinthians 2:16; Philippians 2:5).
- I am the righteousness of God in Jesus Christ (2 Corinthians 5:21).
- I am holy and without blame (Ephesians 1:4; 1 Peter 1:16).
- I am powerful because the Greater One lives in me (1 John 4:4).
- I am limitless. I can do all things through Christ Jesus (Philippians 4:13).
- I am complete in Him (Colossians 2:10).

STEP 4 – Journal

Afterward, take some time to write down what you heard or saw the Holy Spirit speak and show you in your journal.

CHAPTER SIX

The 3rd Big Q: Why Am I Here?

The two most important days in your life are the day
you are born and the day you find out why.
– Mark Twain

If you want to answer the 3rd Big Q: Why am I here? you must first wrap your head around a mind-blowing, heavenly idea. In Christ, your potential is limitless. God's potential is your potential. This is why it is pointless to try to discover your divine destiny until you first discover your divine identity. Knowing who you are in Christ lays the necessary foundation in your heart and mind upon which God can build your life into something that goes beyond your wildest dreams. Without understanding your union with God in Christ, you will never realize your full potential or fulfill your divine destiny.

God's purpose for your life is so much bigger than you. That's why I often call your divine purpose "your bigger-than-you purpose." In fact, your divine purpose is so big, it's going to require God to fulfill it. Your divine purpose, by Divine design, requires something of you, that you, of your own accord, can't do. Your divine purpose is supernatural. Your ability to fulfill God's purpose is based on who God re-created you in Christ to be. This is why the Apostle Paul emphatically stated, "You can do all things *through* Christ (emphasis mine)." I especially like the Amplified version of Philippians 4:13.

> *I can do all things [which He has called me to do] through Him who strengthens and empowers me [to fulfill His purpose – I am self-sufficient in Christ's sufficiency; I am ready for anything and equal to anything through Him who infuses me with inner strength and confident peace].*
> – Philippians 4:13 (AMP)

Through Christ, you have Divine empowerment, the Holy Spirit's power, to overcome any obstacle – physical, spiritual, or otherwise – that would attempt to hinder your life purpose. Without understanding who you are in Christ, however, you will inevitably fall short of reaching your full potential. Your union with God through Christ is what makes the impossible possible.

Not only does believing you are one with God reformat your self-image, it shatters the limitations of what is possible for you to accomplish over the span of your lifetime. It also annihilates the natural constructs and constraints we humans tend to use as excuses to limit what is possible. For example, what does your age have to do with anything when God's involved? How can the balance in your bank accounts dictate what you can or can't do with God?

This is why living out of your true identity in Christ is a necessary prerequisite to purpose. God's plan for your life is bigger than your ability to fulfill it, guaranteed. Besides, a purpose that doesn't require the supernatural isn't Divine in origin. The supernatural aspects of your divine purpose are what make it God-breathed. They also are what require you to maintain a constant connection to God, hence your need to abide in Christ. You simply can't fulfill your *divine* purpose without the Divine's involvement. A life purpose that is possible for you to accomplish wasn't authored by God.

You Were Created for the Supernatural

> *For we are God's [own] handiwork (His workmanship), recreated in Christ Jesus, [born anew] that we may do those good works which God predestined (planned*

*beforehand) for us [taking paths which He prepared ahead of time], that we
should walk in them [living the good life which He prearranged and made ready for
us to live].*
– Ephesians 2:10 (AMPC)

Ephesians 2:10 in the Amplified Classic Translation is another scripture I've been meditating on for a very long time. This powerful verse alludes to just how supernatural God's purpose for your life really is. When it says you were re-created in Christ Jesus to do good works, it is not referring to your ability to do good deeds. Human beings can accomplish good deeds on their own. We can feed the hungry, care for the sick, and take part in all kinds of social justice work. However, when God uses the term "work," it implies a different kind of work. When God refers to work, He is referring to supernatural or miraculous work.

*Heaven and Earth were finished, down to the last detail. By the seventh day God
had finished His work. On the seventh day, He rested from all His work. God
blessed the seventh day. He made it a Holy Day because on that day, He rested
from his work, all the creating God had done. This is the story of how it all started,
of Heaven and Earth when they were created.*
– Genesis 2:1–4 (MSG)

Here, in Genesis, God describes His process of creating heaven and earth as work. Obviously, speaking the world into existence, creating the physical world, and forming Adam out of the dust of the earth was supernatural. Even today, after much progress, mankind is still trying to figure out the origin of the universe and how it works. We have theories and are making new discoveries every day, but the brilliance of the universe is truly mind-boggling.

Jesus also used the word "work" to describe miracles and the supernatural. Amazingly, He encouraged people, if they were having trouble believing He was God, to not just take His word for it, but to believe because of the "work," or in other words, the miracles He was doing.

Just believe that I am in the Father and the Father is in Me. Or at least believe because of the work you have seen Me do. I tell you the truth, anyone who believes in Me will do the same works I have done, and even greater works, because I am going to be with the Father.
– John 14:11–12 (NLT)

But even more incredible, Jesus claimed that anyone who believed in Him would not only do the same kind of work He was doing but also do *even greater works*. This is almost an inconceivable statement that Jesus makes. Jesus healed the sick, cast out devils, raised people from the dead, walked on water, stilled storms, retrieved money out of a fish's mouth, and turned water into wine. And these are just a few of the miracles that were recorded in the Bible. In John 21:25, it says we know only a fraction of the miracles Jesus actually performed.

Jesus also did many other things. If they were all written down, I suppose the whole world could not contain the books that would be written.
– John 21:25 (NLT)

When you are God, obviously there is no limit to the number or kind of miracles you can perform. Yet Jesus said those who believe in Him would do greater works. This sets the bar pretty high, don't you think? Trying to wrap your head around this idea is extremely important, though, if you are going to receive God's purpose for your life. Our idea of dreaming big is minuscule compared to God's idea of dreaming big. But, if you are going to tap into the reason God created you, you are going to have to super-size your expectations. God dreamed something impossibly big for your life.

But, before you get too intimidated, let's continue with Ephesians 2:10. It has more to say about the good works you were re-created in Christ to do. It says these works were "predestined or planned beforehand" for us. The word translated as "predestined" is the Greek word *proorizo*, which means "determine beforehand," "ordain," "to decide upon ahead of time." It also says, in the Amplified Classic Translation, that there were paths that God "prepared ahead of time" so that we could "walk in them" and live "the good life which He prearranged and made ready for us to live."

What I really appreciate about this translation of this verse is how it points out what might not be obvious. Not only did God plan supernatural works as a part of your divine purpose but He also planned the path you are going to need to take to accomplish these works and fulfill your purpose. God's got you covered. There's no reason to freak out about the bigness or impossibility of God's divine purpose for your life. He not only planned your purpose but also planned everything you would need in order to fulfill it. In the end, it won't be you doing the supernatural works that are a part of your purpose, it will be the Father in you that does the work. Like Jesus, God will put the super in your natural.

Do you not believe that I am in the Father and the Father is in Me? The words I say to you, I do not speak on My own. Instead, it is the Father dwelling in Me, carrying out His work.
– John 14:10 (BSB)

Once again, this is why it is imperative that you get established in your true identity and learn to abide in union with the Father through Christ. It is also why there is such a focus on experiencing God in my program, Emerge School of Transformation. Your union with God is the key that unlocks your identity, your destiny, and your full potential. It provides you with the means to do what would otherwise be impossible.

Discovering Your Divine Purpose

I truly believe it is not a coincidence that you are reading this book right now or that the title of this book is *The Path*. My divine purpose is to put people on the path to purpose. The path to purpose is the same, yet entirely unique, for every person on the planet. I know that statement is an oxymoron, but bear with me. The reason the path to purpose is the same for everyone is because Jesus, who calls Himself "The Way," is how you get on the path of purpose. However, once you find yourself in Christ, the path to purpose is as individual as you are. The only way to continue down the individual path God planned for you is to follow Him step by step. This means you have to become proficient at abiding in Christ and hearing from God yourself.

For the remainder of this chapter, I'll be leading you through a series of encounters with God that will help you develop more confidence in your ability to hear from God so that He can reveal aspects of your divine purpose to you. Remember, no one but God can ultimately tell you your divine purpose or empower you to fulfill it. Other people who hear from God can help you hear from Him yourself or possibly help confirm your divine purpose, but in the end, it's between you and your Creator.

Encounter 1 - God's Phone Number

> *Call to Me, and I will answer you, and show you*
> *great and mighty things, which you do not know.*
> – Jeremiah 33:3 (NKJV)

I like to refer to Jeremiah 33:3 as God's phone number. It's a powerful promise that says when we call upon God, He will answer us. In other words, when you need to talk to God, He won't let your call go to voicemail. You've got a direct line to Him that He always picks up. He's always available to you, twenty-four hours a day, seven days a week. I first heard about Jeremiah 33:3 when I didn't have a clue about my life purpose. I also wasn't really sure how to hear from God on demand when I needed to hear Him the most. I was clueless and I was tired of being clueless. I wanted to know my life purpose and answer the question, "Why am I here?" So, I thought, "What the heck, I'll just try it."

One day, after reading Jeremiah 33:3, I started walking around my house yelling out to God. I said, "Hey, God, I'm calling you. In Jeremiah 33:3, you said 'Call upon me and I will answer.'" Almost immediately, I heard the Lord inside of my own thoughts say, "Uh, hello?" I felt pretty ridiculous, but then I heard Him say, "What do you need?" I answered, "I want to know my life purpose. I want to know the reason for my existence."

I remember His response so clearly because it wasn't what I was expecting. He said, "Well, what do you think it is?" I kind of said something that wasn't that great, but then, after a moment of silence, He started talking to me like we were having a normal phone conversation. He said, "For this purpose were you born…" and he began to unpack my life purpose for me. I remember writing it down as He was speaking, amazed at all the things He was sharing.

Now it's your turn. Grab your journal and get ready to call God yourself. I always tell people, if you want to hear God, the least you can do is write it down. I mean, if you really believe you are about to have a conversation with the God of the Universe, don't you think it's worth writing down what He shares with you? Think about it. Don't you usually take a notebook with you to meetings so you don't forget what was discussed? But honestly, I am amazed at how low our expectations can be when it comes to hearing from God. Treat your conversations with God as people did in the Bible. Write them down. If the people in the Bible hadn't written their encounters with God down, we wouldn't have a Bible.

Once you have your journal in front of you, write out Jeremiah 33:3 somewhere on the page. Then do what I did. God is no respecter of persons (Acts 10:34). He'll answer you just like He did me. Stand up and begin to call out to God. Say, "Hello, God. I'm calling you. You said, 'Call to Me and that you would answer and tell me great things, things beyond my ability to imagine, things I could never have known.' Well, I'm calling you. There are some things I want to know about myself. I want to know the answer to some very important questions. Why am I here? What is my life purpose? Pick up the phone please. Show me great things, beyond my ability to imagine, about myself and my life."

I know you may feel a bit strange calling out to God this way, but the Bible is full of people who did strange things. Faith doesn't always make sense. After "calling God" using His phone number, expect Him to answer you. Put the point of your pen down on the paper and just start writing whatever thoughts come to mind. Don't judge your thoughts while you're writing them, just allow them to flow freely like water flowing in a stream. Feel free to make the conversation interactive. If you have questions about something God is sharing with you, ask. If it's helpful, visualize Jesus or the Father on His cell phone having a conversation with you. Write down whatever you see and hear in your journal. You'll be amazed at the "great and mighty things" God shares with you.

Encounter 2 - Experiencing Your Heavenly Persona

For this next encounter, you'll want to find a quiet, comfortable place where you can be alone without interruptions or distractions. Create a peaceful atmosphere. Dim the lights, light a candle, fill the room with flowers, or play soothing music. Then get comfortable. Lie down on the floor or recline in a chair. Settle your mind and open your heart to God. When you are ready, pray the following prayer out loud.

Holy Spirit, I am here today to hear from the Father about my life purpose. Reveal my true identity and show me my divine destiny. As I join you in the Garden of Eden, reveal my heavenly persona. Enlighten my eyes and transform the way I see myself. Show me the things I need to see to understand why the Father created me. Help me understand the reason for my existence. In Jesus' name, AMEN!

After you finish praying, imagine yourself standing in the Garden of Eden, before the fall of man. As you step into the garden, assume a first-person role (as opposed to observing yourself in third person). Engage all of your spiritual senses. What do you see? What do you hear? What do you feel? What do you smell? What do you taste? Spend as much time as necessary taking in the surroundings and feeling the solitude and serenity of the place. When you feel like you're really engaged, ask Jesus to join you.

As He enters, stay focused and engaged in first person. When the time is right, ask Jesus to show you the way the Father created you in the beginning. As you do, shift your perspective to third person so that you are watching yourself and Jesus like a movie. After seeing yourself as you were created to be, assume a first-person perspective and experience your heavenly persona firsthand. Invite the Father to join you and Jesus in the garden. Ask the Father to tell you what He had in mind when He created you. Allow Jesus and the Father to lead you wherever you need to go to understand your divine purpose. Afterward, write down the details of your encounter in your journal.

Encounter 3 - Reading God's Book About You

Psalm 139 is a powerful psalm written by King David. In verses 16–18, he describes how God knew him before he was born and recorded every day of his life in a book.

You saw me before I was born. Every day of my life was recorded in your book. Every moment was laid out before a single day had passed. How precious are your thoughts about me, O God. They cannot be numbered. I can't even count them; they outnumber the grains of sand! And when I wake up, you are still with me!
— Psalms 139:16–18 (NLT)

Like King David, you too have a book that God wrote about your life before you were born. Wouldn't you just love to read God's book about you? Well, you are in luck because that is exactly what this next encounter is all about. As you sit in God's presence, engage your spiritual eyes and imagine you are standing in the Library of Heaven. This library contains all of the books the Father has written about His kids and their lives. Everyone on the planet, from the beginning of human history until its conclusion, has a book in this library. Each book was carefully thought out and written personally by the Father before the person was born, before the world began, in fact.

Using your enlightened eyes, take some time to roam around the Library of Heaven. Visualize it in as much detail as possible in your mind's eye. Engage all of your spiritual senses. What do you hear? What do you smell? Feel the floor underneath your feet and listen for your footsteps as you walk around. Are angels present? What are they doing? Then, when you are ready, find the specific location of your particular book. Hold your book in your hands. Is it heavy or light?

Take your book over to one of the tables or chairs that are located in the library. Spend a few minutes examining the outside of the book. What does it look like? What makes it different from earthly books? What makes it different from all of the other books in the library? When you are ready, open the book and take a look at what the Father has written about you. Is there a particular page or part of your story that reveals the answer to the 3rd Big Q, "Why am I here?" Remember, the book that was written about your life and destiny is supernatural by design. It was created for a supernatural being – the real you. Your book is full of supernatural exploits and impossible dreams come true.

What are some of the supernatural exploits you accomplish in your book? Ask the Holy Spirit what He would like you to discover in the book today. Spend as much time as you would like in the Library of Heaven, reading your book. But remember, you can visit this library anytime. It is open around the clock. Your book will be here for you to read anytime. Just don't forget to write down in your journal the things you see and experience while visiting the library and reading your book. The things God shows you are important clues about your divine purpose.

A Lifestyle of Encounters

Hopefully after having me lead you through each of these encounters, you will have experienced firsthand just how life-transforming encountering God using your spiritual senses actually is. One thing that I've observed after years of leading people through these kinds of spiritual experiences is that what you encounter, you carry. Years ago, during a live Emerge School of Transformation class, one of my students, named Greg, had a powerful experience with Jesus' joy. During the encounter, Greg saw himself as a little boy being thrown in the air over Jesus' head. Greg was having the time of his life, laughing hysterically as Jesus threw him higher and higher. Jesus was laughing right along with Greg. Soon, they both were laughing so hard they fell to the beach, laughing uncontrollably.

When it was time to share with the class, Greg volunteered. As he related the details of his vision to the class, one by one at first, and then everyone all at once, burst out laughing. The joy of Jesus came flooding into the room. We must have laughed for ten minutes. Some students were laughing so hard they literally fell out of their chairs. What in the world? What exactly happened as Greg shared his experience? As I said, what we encounter, we carry. Imaginative prayer may not seem real as you engage in it. It may even feel like you are making up the experiences you are having. Resist the urge to believe this. The spiritual realm is invisible, but absolutely real. What Greg experienced with Jesus in his imagination was a real spiritual experience. So real, in fact, that it affected the entire atmosphere of the classroom when he shared it.

Time does not permit me to share the countless stories from students and others who have encountered God in the ways you are learning in this book. Students have prayed for others halfway around the world while engaging with Jesus in imaginative prayer and have seen them instantaneously healed. Others have been shown the future exactly as it would play out in their lives. The experiences you have during imaginative prayer are powerful. Don't underestimate the encounters you are having with God. Experiences with God are transformative and required if you are to discover your answer to "Why am I here?" and fulfill your divine purpose.

Love Letter from God

My Purpose-Filled Child,

The day you were born filled my heart with such joy. Finally, your time had come. All of heaven rejoiced with Me. My masterpiece was being revealed to the world. As I watched you grow, evolve, and search for significance unaware of My presence most days, I would sing songs of victory over you and declare your divine destiny to the four corners of the earth. At night while you slept, I would give you dreams that would cultivate your life purpose and cause the eternity I planted in your heart to spring forth. Day by day, I saw you approaching this moment. In the waiting, I worked things together for your good.

Today, as you "dig deeper," I will be digging with you. Together we will mine our hearts that have become one. I will be with you every step of the way, guiding you down the path. As we walk hand in hand, I will speak to you clearly. Now is the time for you to discover the reason you were born. I haven't been hiding your purpose from you. I've been keeping it safe for you. But now is the time. You are ready, child. I can't wait to reveal all that I have prepared. My purpose for you is blissfully divine.

Trust that as you seek Me, you will hear Me clearly. My voice will infuse your thoughts. My Spirit will inspire your imagination. Believe what you are hearing is directly from Me. I want you to be confident that you hear from Me. I will never leave you, nor will I forsake you. I am with you now and forever, with you every moment, in every breath. I will continue down the path of purpose with you. Walking in you and beside you until all is fulfilled.

Kisses from Heaven,
Dad

Digging Deeper Exercises - Discovering Your Divine Purpose

Exercise 1 - Receiving Your Very Own "I Am" Statements

The Gospel of John contains seven statements Jesus spoke about himself. These were no ordinary statements. They were statements that described Jesus' unique identity and divine purpose. They reveal Jesus' answers to the 2nd and 3rd Big Qs – "Who am I?" and "Why am I here?"

Recognize that the use of the words "I Am" in Jesus' statements is not accidental. It is a reference back to Exodus 3:13–15 where God revealed Himself to Abraham as the great I AM THAT I AM. It was in response to the Pharisees' question "Who do you think you are?" that Jesus said,

"'Your father Abraham rejoiced at the thought of seeing my day; he saw it and was glad.' 'You are not yet fifty years old,' the Jews said to him, 'and you have seen Abraham!' 'I tell you the truth,' Jesus answered, 'before Abraham was born, I am!' At this, they picked up stones to stone him, but Jesus hid himself, slipping away from the temple grounds."
– John 8:56–59

The violent response of the Jews to Jesus' "I Am" statement indicates they clearly understood what He was declaring – that He was the eternal God incarnate. Jesus was equating Himself with the "I Am" title God gave Himself in Exodus 3:14. The reason that this is so significant, beyond the fact that Jesus is God come in the flesh, is that Jesus was speaking out of who He believed He was. He was declaring His heavenly persona. He wasn't merely saying, "I am the son of Joseph and Mary," which was his earthly persona. He was boldly and confidently living out of His true identity and who the Father declared Him to be.

Jesus' Seven "I Am" Declarations

- And Jesus said to them, "I am the bread of life. He who comes to Me shall never hunger, and he who believes in Me shall never thirst" (John 6:35).

- Then Jesus spoke to them again, saying, "I am the light of the world. He who follows Me shall not walk in darkness, but have the light of life" (John 8:12).
- "I am the door. If anyone enters by Me, he will be saved, and will go in and out and find pasture" (John 10:9).
- "I am the good shepherd. The good shepherd gives His life for the sheep" (John 10:11).
- Jesus said to her, "I am the resurrection and the life. He who believes in Me, though he may die, he shall live" (John 11:25).
- Jesus said to him, "I am the way, the truth, and the life. No one comes to the Father except through Me" (John 14:6).
- "I am the true vine, and My Father is the vinedresser" (John 15:1).

Now it's your turn. Like Jesus, you are going to spend time with the Father uncovering your own "I Am" statements. Ideally, you should have no more than seven "I Am" identity statements, just like Jesus.

STEP 1 - Set the Atmosphere
Find a quiet place where you can be alone and focus.
- Set aside a few moments to get yourself in the right frame of mind.
- The goal is to clear your mind of distractions and connect with your spirit.
- Consider having soft, worshipful music playing in the background or lighting a candle.

Once you feel connected and can sense God's presence, you're ready to move to the next step.

STEP 2 - Start a Fresh Page in Your Journal
Start a fresh page in your journal with nothing on it but today's date and the following opening statement.

Father, speak to my heart about who you created me to be. From your perspective, how would you describe me?

- Imagine the Father sitting with you as you journal.
- Use your spiritual eyes as you journal.
- Alternate between seeing, hearing, and asking questions.
- Whatever the Father speaks, write it down in your journal.

As you write, remain open to spiritual imagery. Jesus' identity statements included inanimate objects such as bread and light. Recognize that the Father may show you "you" through nature, animals, or really anything. Allow the Father to show you the meaning behind the inanimate object and how that relates to your divine purpose. For example, bread nourishes and light shines. Consider looking up the definition of the words the Father gives you to help you understand the significance of what the Father is speaking to you.

STEP 3 – Ask the Father to Reveal Something to You about Your Name

Continue your conversation with the Father asking Him to reveal something to you about your name. Google your name to see what it means. As you explore the meaning of your name, remain open to hearing the Father explain or change your name. Remember, Abraham, Peter, and Paul all received new names from the Lord. If your name has a meaning related to an object in the same way Simon meant "reed" and Peter meant "rock," look up the definitions of the word. This will help you better understand the significance of what the Father is speaking to you.

STEP 4 – Write Down Everything the Father Shows You in Your Journal

- Take copious notes.
- These words from the Father are pure gold.
- And, because it's the Father speaking them to you, these are no ordinary words.
- They are filled with the power to bring themselves to pass (think, "Let there be light.").

STEP 5 - Review Your Words from the Father

- Gather different colored pens, pencils, and/or highlighters.
- Take a few moments to read back over everything you've written in your journal so far.
- As you read, highlight key phrases and words that jump out at you or seem significant.
- Organize these words and phrases on a new page in your journal.

STEP 6 - Pray and Form Your "I Am" Statements

- Ask the Holy Spirit to highlight your highlights.
- Ask Him to show you which phrases and words you are to use as the basis for your "I Am" statements.
- Begin to form the phrases and words into first-person "I Am" declarations.

STEP 7 - Finalize and Meditate on Your "I Am" Statements

Write out your "I Am" statements clearly and concisely on four- by six-inch index cards, one per card.

- Use Jesus' statements as a guide.
- Read each of your "I Am" statements aloud over yourself.
- Visualize each "I Am" statement as you read it.
- Jot down things the Father shows you about each "I Am" statement in your journal.
- Speak your "I Am" statement over yourself frequently.
- Stick with it until they feel real.

Exercise 2 - Walking Down Memory Lane

In this exercise, you are going to allow the Holy Spirit to lead you back through time and help you remember the specific instances in your life where He was awakening a desire within you to know your purpose. The memories, whether you realized it at the time or not, were defining moments in your life that provide specific clues about your divine purpose. Some may feel like the wake-up calls I described on my path to purpose, others may have caused you to believe something specifically related to your divine purpose or to realize that you needed to head in a different direction because you weren't living a life of purpose.

STEP 1 - Get "Still" Before the Lord

Find a quiet place where you can be alone and focus.

- Set aside a few moments to get yourself in the right frame of mind.
- The goal is to clear your mind of distractions and connect with your spirit.
- Consider having soft worshipful music playing in the background or lighting a candle.

Once you feel connected and can sense God's presence, you're ready to move to the next step.

STEP 2 - Ask the Holy Spirit to Help

Pray the following prayer out loud:

Holy Spirit, Thank You for Your presence. Thank You for Your love. And most of all, thank You for being You! Today, we're going to take a walk down memory lane. As we do, I'm asking You to do what You do best. Lead and guide me into the truth. Reveal Yourself and speak to my heart. Bring the things to my remembrance that You want me to recall. Help me connect the dots of my life and make sense of my journey. Help me recognize the ways that You've been nudging me awake and planting the desire in my heart to know my purpose and find the answer to the question "Why am I here?" Bring up relevant memories and life-defining experiences that reveal my life purpose. Show me how you've been working in my life – prompting me to ask "why" and dig deeper. In Jesus' name, AMEN!

STEP 3 – Journal Time

Start a new page in your journal and ask the Holy Spirit to begin to reveal specific memories that would be considered defining moments in your life and provide clues about your divine purpose.

- As you remember each instance, write down the memory in as much detail as you can.
- How did you feel?
- What was the significance of the experience?
- How did the experience shape and direct your life?
- What did you learn?
- What decisions did you make as a result of the experience?
- Ask the Holy Spirit to reveal how this experience is connected to your life purpose.
- What does He want you to learn about your purpose through the experience?
- Ask the Holy Spirit what else He wants to speak to you about this memory.
- Write down as many memories as the Holy Spirit brings up.

STEP 4 – Create a Memory Map

In this step, you are going to "connect the dots." Starting with another new page in your journal, create a box for each memory and give the memory a name. In each box, summarize how this experience provided clues to your life purpose. Write down key words and phrases about the experience that are related to your life purpose.

STEP 5 – Connecting the Dots

Once your memory map is complete, ask the Holy Spirit to help you identify the overall themes and patterns that seemed to repeat themselves over the course of your life. Try to find at least six themes and patterns. If you can't find six, ask the Holy Spirit to reveal other memories that are relevant to your life purpose and revisit steps 3 and 4.

Write down simple phrases for each theme or pattern that express, summarize, and best describe it. As an example, here are the phrases I use to describe my life story:

1. I hate religion
2. Authenticity in everything
3. Uniqueness is key
4. Leadership comes naturally
5. Influence through communication
6. Truth sets you free

Once you've identified at least six phrases, it is time to narrow them down. Read over each phrase to see if any are similar enough to be combined with one another. For example, two of my phrases – "authenticity in everything" and "uniqueness is key" – are similar enough to be combined into one phrase. I chose "be authentic and unique." It's important not to overthink this part of the exercise. Trust your gut and think about the meaning of the words. Write down in your journal the six phrases you identify.

STEP 6 – Formulating a Life Purpose Statement

Once you have the six phrases identified, take some time to reflect on each one. Ask the Holy Spirit how the statement applies to your life purpose. Then, when you feel ready, taking all of the encounters and work you've completed in this chapter, take a stab at writing a life purpose statement for your life.

As you craft your life purpose statement remember to keep it simple. In Emerge, we use the following format, but feel free to use whatever structure feels best.

My life purpose is to: _____

So that: _____.

Your life purpose statement can incorporate one of your "I Am" statements or describe something else God showed you. The "so that" portion of your life purpose statement should describe the impact your life is destined to have in the world.

Here are a few examples of life purpose statements that Emergers have written.

- My life purpose is to be the voice of love so that God's true nature is revealed to the world.
- My life purpose is to be a safe place for the broken so that they can experience God's healing power.
- My life purpose is to be the light that shines in the darkest of places so that Jesus is revealed to people who wouldn't be able to find him otherwise.
- My life purpose is to reveal God's beauty so that people experience what heaven is like.
- My life purpose is to create wealth so that poverty becomes a thing of the past.

As you formulate your life purpose, make sure you give yourself grace. You aren't writing the words in stone. It's fine to treat it as a work in progress. As you walk down the path that leads to your destiny, you will learn more about who you are and what you were created to do. You can always refine your life purpose statement as things become more clear.

CHAPTER SEVEN

The 4th Big Q: Where Am I Headed?

If you don't know where you are going, any road will get you there.
— Lewis Carroll

You weren't born to just take up space. God has a vision for your life. Just like Jesus, you were sent into this world for a specific purpose. His vision for your life is the *how* and *what* that goes hand in hand with your *why*. It describes how you are going to fulfill your purpose and what you are called to specifically accomplish during your lifetime. It is the answer to the question, "Where am I headed?" God's vision for your life unveils your divine destiny and shows you the end of your life before you live it. It describes how your purpose will manifest and how He plans to reveal His glory through you over the course of your life.

It Is Finished

Your birth is proof that you are needed on this planet. It is the first step in the fulfillment of God's purpose for your life. Although mind-boggling to think about, God dreamed of you long before you were born, actually, before anyone was born. You were in God's heart, resting in Christ, before the foundation of the world. This means that before the Father said, "Let there be light," you already existed in the mind of God. Actually, there are many things from God's perspective that were "finished" before time began.

- God, Himself, existed before the foundation of the world (Genesis 1:1, Psalm 90:2, Isaiah 41:21).
- Christ existed before the foundation of the world (Isaiah 48:16, Micah 5:2, John 1:1, John 17:5, John 17:23).
- Christ was loved by the Father before the foundation of the world (John 17:24).
- Wisdom was established before the foundation of the world (Proverbs 8:23).
- You were chosen in Christ before the foundation of the world (Ephesians 1:4).
- God saved you and called you holy before the foundation of the world (2 Timothy 1:9).
- God promised eternal life before time began (Titus 1:2).
- God foreknew you and predestined you to be conformed to the image of Jesus (Romans 8:29).
- Christ was chosen as our ransom before the world began (1 Peter 1:20, Revelation 13:8).
- The lamb of God, Jesus, was slain before the foundation of the world (Revelation 13:8).
- Unrevealed secrets of God existed from the foundation of the world (Matthew 13:35).
- The Kingdom of God, our inheritance, was prepared for us before the creation of the world (Matthew 13:35).
- The blood of the all the prophets was shed from the foundation of the world (Luke 11:50).

Wrapping your head about all of the things that were finished from God's perspective before creation requires that you radically adjust your perspective. The gospel was not God's plan B that He thought of in response to humankind's sin. The gospel was God's original plan. God predetermined Jesus' destiny before the foundation of the world. Peter wrote, "He was chosen before the foundation of the world but was revealed at the end of the times for you" (1 Peter 1:20). The Son was designed as the lamb of God by the Father before the beginning of time. From God's perspective, Jesus was crucified before He was born. When Jesus was born, at the appointed time in history, He simply fulfilled God's vision within the context of time. Galatians 4:4 says, "When the time came to completion, God sent His Son." When the right time came, Jesus fulfilled what from God's perspective had already been accomplished.

Finishing What's Already Finished

Before His crucifixion, in John 17, Jesus prays an incredible prayer to the Father, which sheds more light on the subject.

> *When Jesus had spoken these things, He lifted up His eyes to heaven and said, Father, the hour has come. Glorify and exalt and honor and magnify Your Son, so that Your Son may glorify and extol and honor and magnify You. [Just as] You have granted Him power and authority over all flesh (all humankind), [now glorify Him] so that He may give eternal life to all whom You have given Him. And this is eternal life: [it means] to know (to perceive, recognize, become acquainted with, and understand) You, the only true and real God, and [likewise] to know Him, Jesus [as the] Christ (the Anointed One, the Messiah), Whom You have sent. I have glorified You down here on the earth by completing the work that You gave Me to do. And now, Father, glorify Me along with Yourself and restore Me to such majesty and honor in Your presence as I had with You before the world existed. I have manifested Your Name [I have revealed Your very Self, Your real Self] to the people whom You have given Me out of the world. They were Yours, and You gave them to Me, and they have obeyed and kept Your word. Now [at last] they know and understand that all You have given Me belongs to You [is really and truly Yours]. For the [uttered] words that You gave Me I have given them; and they have received and accepted [them] and have come to know positively and in reality [to believe with absolute assurance] that I came forth from Your presence, and they have believed and are convinced that You did send Me.*
>
> *– John 17:1–8 (AMPC)*

There is so much revelation jam-packed in these verses. In verse 4, Jesus says He has glorified the Father through His life by finishing the work the Father had given Him to accomplish. What work? The work He describes in verses 6 through 7. Jesus manifested the Father and showed people what He was really like. What's important to realize about all of this, however, is that Jesus finishing the work the Father had given Him to accomplish was the fulfillment of what God had determined before the beginning of time.

When you put this in the context of Ephesians 2:10, which we spent some time looking at while tackling the 3rd Big Q – "Why am I here?" – it makes even more sense.

> *For we are God's [own] handiwork (His workmanship), recreated in Christ Jesus, [born anew] that we may do those good works which God predestined (planned beforehand) for us [taking paths which He prepared ahead of time], that we should walk in them [living the good life which He prearranged and made ready for us to live].*
> *– Ephesians 2:10 (AMPC)*

Jesus, in His prayer to the Father in John 17, was in effect saying, "Father, I finished the good works which You predestined and planned before time for Me to do. I have walked down the path that You prepared for Me ahead of time." Jesus' life was the fulfillment of God's preordained plan for His life. This is why Jesus could say at the moment of His death, "It is finished" (John 19:30). In that moment, the lamb who had been slain from the Father's perspective from the foundation of the world was now slain from everyone else's perspective.

A New Perspective

The reason it is imperative that you understand the Father's perspective about the life of Jesus – that it was done before He was born – is because the same is true about God's vision for your life. The good works that the Father planned for your life have already been completed from His perspective. He already sees you as being the person who accomplished them. He sees the vision for your life fulfilled. All that is left to do is for you to receive God's vision for your life, walk down the paths He's prepared for you, and live the good life He prearranged and made ready for you to live. This is why we spent time in the last chapter visiting the Library of Heaven. God's story for your life is His vision for your life. The book about your life described in Psalms 139:16–18 is finished. He wrote it before you were born – before the beginning of time.

Understanding that God's vision for your life is finished from His perspective is incredibly empowering. It takes the pressure off of you to have to make something happen. You simply need to surrender to what has already been established in God's heart for you. You don't have to force your purpose to be fulfilled. You can simply enjoy the journey of walking down the path that leads to the manifestation of your purpose, delighting in the Father's company. You can also trust that God's vision for your life fits you to a tee. Everything about you, from the way you look, your personality, the things that you are good at, to the things that you enjoy are by Divine design. God didn't come up with His vision for your life without who He created you to be in mind. He dreamed up His vision for your life as a means for you to fully express the glory He placed in you. The things He has called you to accomplish are designed to authentically express the fullness of who you are in Him. In fact, the more you learn to settle into your own skin and rest in who He created you to be, the sooner you'll manifest His vision for your life. It's trying to be someone that we aren't or that we think we should be that's exhausting.

God's Vision for You Is Awesome

God doesn't expect you to do anything that doesn't come naturally to you, through the grace that rests on your life. He's not going to call you to be something you hate or have no passion to do. That's not how love works. Love doesn't seek its own. It isn't selfish. Love desires what is best for others. God's vision for your life is your best life. It's a life that you will look back on with joy and gratitude for having the privilege of living it. God's vision for your life reveals you at your very best. It involves you doing something you are amazing at and love to do. The critical voice in your head criticizing you, discouraging you, and telling you all the reasons why you can't follow your heart and fulfill your potential is not the voice of Love. It is not the voice of God. It's the voice of religion, performance, and legalism and it's exhausting trying to be good enough to get it to shut up.

But this is one of the reasons the gospel is such good news. When we get to know Jesus, we can rest and simply trust the Holy Spirit to reveal God's plan for our life to us. We can also trust Him to fulfill His plan through us. Faithful is He who called you, He will also do it (1 Thessalonians 5:24).

Getting Off the Performance Treadmill

Are you tired? Worn out? Burned out on religion? Come to me. Get away with me and you'll recover your life. I'll show you how to take a real rest. Walk with me and work with me — watch how I do it. Learn the unforced rhythms of grace. I won't lay anything heavy or ill-fitting on you. Keep company with me and you'll learn to live freely and lightly.
– Matthew 11:28–30 (MSG)

Matthew 11:28–30 in the Message Translation is one of my favorite translations of this verse. Whether we realize it or not, religion is what is always trying to get us to be something we are not. The name of the game that runs the world, which is a manifestation of the religious spirit, is *performance*. No matter how hard you work, no matter how hard you try, you can never measure up to the standard of perfection that the world requires. Eat healthy, work out, be a good parent, be a good spouse, be a good friend, save money, invest money, pay your taxes, work hard but not too hard, keep your house clean, volunteer your time, go to church, tell the truth, form good habits – the list goes on and on. Life is exhausting when we try to live up to the expectations of what it means to be a good person.

Thank God that in Christ, we have been set free from the law and performance. We now are free to dance with the Father to the "unforced rhythms of grace." Fulfilling God's vision for your life is something He does through you, by His grace. When Jesus says, "Walk with me and work with me – watch how I do it. Learn the unforced rhythms of grace," it's important to remember how Jesus fulfilled God's vision for His life. He lived in union with the Father (John 10:30). The Father in Him did the work (John 14:10). He spoke the words that the Father gave Him to speak (John 12:49). He went so far as to say, "I can do nothing in my own self."

So Jesus explained, "I tell you the truth, the Son can do nothing by Himself. He does only what He sees the Father doing. Whatever the Father does, the Son also does. For the Father loves the Son and shows Him everything He is doing. In fact, the Father will show Him how to do even greater works than healing this man. Then you will truly be astonished."
– John 5:19–20 (NLT)

How refreshing is this? If Jesus couldn't do anything on His own, then how helpless are we?

Receiving God's Vision for Your Life

Dreams are seeds of possibility planted in your soul, calling you to pursue a unique path to the realization of your purpose.
– John Maxwell

The process for receiving God's vision for your life is actually the same process I've been sharing throughout this book. You simply ask God to show it to you. If you have worked through the Digging Deeper Exercises laid out at the end of each chapter, then you are ready to answer the 4th Big Q: "Where am I headed?" The most important advice I can give you is simply to surrender your life to God. When you let go of your life, you find it (remember Matthew 10:39?). The only other thing that is really required is for you to spend time with God, dreaming. God is a big dreamer. He's so fun to dream with. And because there's not a religious bone in His body, He cares about every single one of your dreams. All of your dreams matter to God. Yes, the 4th Big Q is about discovering God's vision for your life, but all of your dreams are important. God is first and foremost your Father. Yes, you are called to make a difference in the world, but you are also called to enjoy life.

My purpose is to give them a rich and satisfying life.
– John 10:10 (NLT)

Let's look at this scripture in the Amplified Version as well.

> *I came that they may have and enjoy life, and have it in abundance*
> *[to the full, till it overflows].*
> – John 10:10 (AMP)

Jesus came so that we would enjoy life! Isn't this amazing? The Creator of the Universe, God Almighty, your Heavenly Father, wants you to live a rich and satisfying life. Do you know what this means? You are supposed to have fun! You are to live life to the fullest and pursue the dreams in your heart! The Father is interested in every aspect of your life, not just the "spiritual" things or the things that serve other people. Every aspect of your life – your personality, your passions, your dreams, and your life experiences – all contribute to who God made you to be. Even the things that seem like a big waste of time – your biggest failures, mistakes, and disappointments – can be used by God for good.

But here's the thing that most people don't connect with when they think about their life. Our dreams reflect who God created us to be. Let me say that another way. Your dreams are a reflection of your true identity. Every dream and desire in your heart carries the potential to reveal the goodness of God. He loves the things you are passionate about. He made you that way! Our Father is passionate about everything! He loves sports, ballet, art, travel, archery – you name it! He's a man of many talents! Here's the deal, the Father doesn't look at things the way the spirit of religion has taught us that He does. He doesn't categorize things as spiritual or natural, sacred or secular. That's a Western or Greek mind-set, it is not God's. The Hebrew or Eastern way of thinking recognizes that all of life is connected and interwoven. This is how the Father thinks as well. To the Father, everything is a revelation of Him!

The problem is that religion has so distorted and clouded our perception of the Father that we don't see Him as the fun Dad that He really is. As a result, we conform ourselves to an image of what we think we are supposed to look like rather than walk in the freedom to be exactly who God created us to be. Jesus came to reveal a Father who is so in love with you, so unbelievably good to you, and so abundantly generous with you, that you would run into His arms and never leave.

You living out the dreams in your heart is exactly the testimony the world needs. It shows the world the kind of Dad you have. Your dreams are one of the purest reflections of the Father's true identity. Let me say that again. Your dreams are one of the purest reflections of your Father's true identity. When you live out your dreams, you glorify your Father. So, what kind of dreams glorify God? How about ending world hunger, becoming the first female president, or giving away a billion dollars? Big dreams like these absolutely glorify God. But so do fun dreams like riding a camel, swimming with dolphins, or learning how to walk a tightrope. Seemingly frivolous dreams such as these glorify God by revealing His fun side. God is a fun Dad. He loves to do fun things with you. He is first and foremost relational, that's why He revealed Himself through Jesus as Father. It's also why He loves the dreams you have for your relationships – to be an amazing parent, friend, and leader. He also loves it when you set goals that enable you to reach your dreams, like graduating from college or learning a new language. All of your dreams, no matter how big or small, glorify God when they come true.

This is why in Emerge, I spend a lot of time working with students to help them expand their capacity to dream. I actually take them through a dream-storming exercise where they have to write down 100 dreams that they would like to accomplish in their lifetime. It's amazing to see how much resistance many students have to overcome to dream 100 dreams. This exercise forces them to go beyond their internal setpoint and explore more of what is actually inside their hearts. For many, it is the first time they've ever given themselves permission to dream. For most, it is an absolutely necessary first step to receiving God's vision for their lives. It stretches their capacity to dream so that they can receive God's really big dream that manifests their purpose in life.

Now It's Your Turn

There's something specific God had in mind when He created you that only you, through the power of His Spirit, can accomplish. Discovering God's vision for your life means you are going to have to set the inner dreamer inside of you free. You are going to have to give yourself permission to believe God is better than anything you've imagined and cares more than anyone else about you living a full and satisfying life. Your ability to receive God's vision for your life is directly related to your ability to dream God-sized dreams – dreams that seem impossible without God fulfilling them.

In the Digging Deeper Exercise at the end of the chapter, I am going to challenge you to dream bigger than you've ever dreamed before. It's important that you take the time you need to really mine your heart and connect with the things that will make your life extraordinary. You weren't created to live a mundane, boring life. Life in the kingdom is meant to be an adventure. I encourage you, as you work through the Digging Deeper Exercise, to also revisit the Library of Heaven and read more of what the Father dreamed for you before the beginning of time. If you do that, I bet that you'll find at least one chapter in your book that is dedicated to your dreams and you receiving God's vision for your life.

In my own life, I can attest to the reality of God's dream for your life being bigger, better, and more fulfilling than anything you could ever imagine on your own. It's simply miraculous how He weaves your past into your future and uses all of your life experiences, even the worst ones, to make your life so beautiful that it takes your breath away. He is a master builder, a masterpiece maker, who makes everything beautiful in its own time.

He has made everything beautiful in its time.
He has also set eternity in the human heart.
Ecclesiastes 3:11 (NIV)

Love Letter from God

My Glorious Child,

Climb up on my lap and see the key to your heart that I wear as a locket around my neck. I wear it as a reminder so that every time you give me a hug, you'll remember that I've set your heart free. You are free to dream. You are free to fly. You are free to be all that I've created you to be. There is absolutely no fear in My love which means you are free to live fearlessly. Fear of failure, fear of greatness, fear of lack, and fear of Me were just a few of the fears that were swallowed up in Jesus' victory. My love never fails. The Greater One now lives in you. My abundance is your inheritance. You now live and move and have your being inside of Me. What on earth is there to fear?

I've called you to expand My kingdom of heaven on the earth. My vision is for Perfect Love to rule the world. You have an incredible part to play in heaven's invasion of the earth. My dream for you is a part of My dream for the human race. The work I have given you is not designed to feel like toil. It's designed to feel like breathing and dancing – effortless and fun. You have My permission to quit being someone I didn't create you to be. If there are things in your life that feel like they don't fit, stop wearing them. My vision for your life fits you perfectly. It is comfortable and lightweight, not itchy or ill-fitting.

Don't pursue a life that you think will please Me. I'm already pleased with you. Listen to your heart. It beats to the rhythm of My grace. Marching to the beat of your own drum isn't optional if you are to fulfill all that I've predestined for you. If you can't be yourself, then who will you be? It's you being you that thrills My heart and glorifies Me the most. So close your eyes, beloved, and dream big with Me. If all things are really possible, what on earth do you want to be?

Kisses from Heaven,
Dad

Digging Deeper Exercise – A Picture Is Worth a Thousand Words

In this Digging Deeper Exercise, we are going to be creating a Life Vision Board that is a tangible, visual representation of God's vision for your life. Creating a Life Vision Board helps you receive and remember your vision. Because our minds respond strongly to visual images, creating a Life Vision Board is a simple, yet powerful way to "see" God's vision for your life. It is a tangible representation of who God has created you to be and helps you envision the life He planned for you before the foundation of the world.

In its simplest form, a Life Vision Board is a collection of pictures, words, scriptures, and inspirational phrases arranged on a poster board that depict God's vision for your life. It should include some of the ways that you will express your life's true intent, inspire others, and make a difference in the world. In effect, it synchronizes your physical eyes with your spiritual eyes, acting as a visual reminder of what you are called to accomplish in your life.

As you focus on your Life Vision Board and meditate on it regularly, you will find your mind "catching up" with your spirit. Your self-image will be transformed as you spend dedicated time focusing on how God sees you. You'll also find your life purpose – your *why* – and your life vision – your *how* – coming alive in your heart like never before. As a result, you'll find your life supernaturally shifting and aligning with God's plans and purposes. The principle of scripture in Proverbs 23:7 that says, "As a man thinks in his heart so is he," will spring into action. You will find yourself taking steps that once seemed difficult or even impossible with a new level of confidence. As you continue to believe and act in agreement with your Life Vision Board, you'll find the seen realm responding and aligning with the things you've placed on your Life Vision Board.

You have been created in the image of the Creator. You were designed by the Father to dream, imagine, and visualize the impossible and then partner with Him to bring it to pass. Therefore, what you meditate on matters. The words that you speak matter. Like our Father's, both our thoughts and words are creative. Here are just a few verses that speak of the power of our thoughts and words.

Keep your heart with all vigilance, for from it flow the springs of life.
— Proverbs 4:23 (ESV)

Death and life are in the power of the tongue.
— Proverbs 18:21 (ESV)

I tell you, on the day of judgment people will give account for every careless word they speak, for by your words you will be justified, and by your words you will be condemned.
— Matthew 12:36–37 (ESV)

And now I commend you to God and to the word of his grace, which is able to build you up...
— Acts 20:32 (ESV)

Let no corrupting talk come out of your mouths, but only such as is good for building up, as fits the occasion, that it may give grace to those who hear.
— Ephesians 4:29 (ESV)

Finally, brothers, whatever is true, whatever is honorable, whatever is just, whatever is pure, whatever is lovely, whatever is commendable, if there is any excellence, if there is anything worthy of praise, think about these things.
— Philippians 4:8 (ESV)

Whoever desires to love life and see good days, let him keep his tongue from evil and his lips from speaking deceit.
— 1 Peter 3:10 (ESV)

Beloved, I pray that you may prosper in all things and be in health, just as your soul prospers.
— 1 John 3:2 (NKJV)

Creating a Life Vision Board is not just a natural exercise. It's a sacred, supernatural one. It evokes the spiritual law of attraction. This scriptural principle teaches that our thoughts and words attract and create the very things we think about and speak. We were called to be imitators of God (Ephesians 5:1), and God never intended for us to think or speak negatively. God expects us to act as He does. He expects us to think and speak of nonexistent things as though they already exist (Romans 4:17, Amplified Version).

The book of Genesis reveals how in the beginning, God transformed the darkness into light by simply saying, "Let there be light." He didn't meditate, think, or speak about darkness. He spoke in alignment with what He intended to create. In the same way, we are not to meditate, think, or speak about the things we want to see transformed in our life. Instead, we are to speak them into existence. However, our words always reflect what is in our heart – the things we truly believe. Therefore, if we desire to transform our speech, we must first transform our hearts. We must transform what we believe and upgrade our thought life. This is where a Life Vision Board comes in.

Meditating on your Life Vision Board is a supernatural exercise. Visualizing yourself as the person God has created you to be, doing the things He created you to do causes you to believe it. In fact, it's so powerful, it works regardless of whether you understand why. Olympic athletes have been using the power of visualization for decades to improve performance. Scientific studies have proven that the exact same brain patterns were activated when a weightlifter imagined lifting weights as when they actually lifted them.

Creating a Life Vision Board is a fun and fulfilling undertaking, especially when you approach the project with child-like faith. Think back to doing art as a child or a time when you enjoyed being creative. There is only one major rule to creating a Life Vision Board, and it's that there aren't any rules. You aren't going to mess it up; you can create your Life Vision Board however you feel led. It's your life vision, after all. You feel the deepest desires of your heart most intensely. The only real secret to creating a vision board that works is to focus on how it makes you feel.

When you look at your Life Vision Board, it should elicit your emotions and feed your faith. Your response should feel visceral. It should inspire you, motivate you, and stir up passion. It should awaken your spirit and cause you to transcend what is rational or natural. I know this may sound like a tall order for something as simple as a Life Vision Board, but remember, you won't be alone in this exercise. The Holy Spirit is your Helper. He will be there with you, within you, helping you create a vision board that reflects the Father's heart for you.

Don't be surprised if He uses the process of creating a Life Vision Board to heal your heart or reveal Himself to you in very deep and meaningful ways. I'm sure when the Father was talking with Abraham about the stars and sharing His heart about His desire for childless Abraham to father a multitude, Abraham got a little emotional. Our life purpose taps into our deepest desires, and desire, by definition, is emotional.

Hopefully, by this point you've recognized that God is an emotional God who loves to express Himself. He feels things deeply. He is motivated by compassion and angered at injustice. His emotions aren't something He avoids or suppresses. Jesus wept at the tomb of Lazarus and angrily cleared the temple after seeing the money changers. Therefore, don't be afraid of the feelings that surface during this exercise. Embrace them. They are designed by God and will help you confirm your life purpose. Your true life purpose will always be something you are deeply passionate about.

STEP 1 - Gather Materials

Before creating your Life Vision Board, you'll want to gather the following materials:

- Any kind of board: A cork board, poster board, or pin board works best. I personally like to use the trifold ones that you can purchase at your local Target, Walmart, or office supplies store. However, cork boards from the hardware store are also great. If you are looking for a more decorative alternative or something pretty to look at, feel free and go for it.
- Scissors, tape, pins, or a glue-stick to put your board together.
- If you want, fun markers, stickers, or anything else you can think of to deck out your board. I don't use those, but if embellishments make you feel great, then go for it.
- Images and quotes from magazines or the Internet.
- Most importantly, the stuff you want to look at every day.

- Photos, quotes, sayings, images of places you want to go, reminders of events, places, or people, postcards from friends, and just about anything that will inspire you.

STEP 2 – Set the Mood

Before jumping into creating your Life Vision Board, take the time to set the atmosphere.

- You will want to set aside a couple of distraction-free hours to put your board together.
- Turn off the TV and turn on some relaxing, worshipful music.
- Light a candle and clear your space.
- Spend 5–10 minutes in quiet reflection.
- Pray in the Spirit or simply worship.
- The goal is to clear your mind.

As always, have your journal with you. The Holy Spirit might have some things to speak to you about His vision for your life and your Life Vision Board or to help you clear your mind.

STEP 3 – Assembling Your Life Vision Board

Once you're in the right mind-set, follow these simple steps:

- Begin to gather pictures that represent or symbolize your answer to the 3rd Big Q, "Why am I here?"
- Include your Life Mission Statement.
- Choose images that convey the experiences, feelings, desires, and dreams God has placed in your heart.
- Use photographs, magazine cutouts, or pictures from the Internet.
- Find what inspires you and be creative.
- Include not only pictures but anything that speaks to you.
- Consider artistically designing your name and including a photograph of yourself.
- Add affirmations, inspirational words, scriptures, quotes – words that inspire you.
- Dream big and include visions for your future.

- Get creative. Paste a picture of your head on someone else doing what you are dreaming of doing.
- Ask the Holy Spirit to join in. He loves to show you your future. He will help you include things that cause you to see yourself fulfilling your life vision.

When it comes to actually assembling the board, some people like to leave space in between each item. However, if you love the feeling of closeness and want everything to touch and overlap, then huddle it all together and overlap your objects. As for choosing what makes the final cut, lay everything out before you start gluing and pinning so you can get an idea of where you want everything. Remember to use only words and images that best represent your purpose and life vision. Everything on your Life Vision Board should inspire you and build your faith. Consider including your "I Am" statements. Draw from the 2nd and 3rd Big Qs as appropriate.

STEP 4 – Using Your Life Vision Board

After your Life Vision Board is complete, place it somewhere you will see it frequently. I encourage you to spend a few minutes daily meditating on your Life Vision Board. In addition, if you can spend at least 15 minutes of dedicated time meditating on your Life Vision Board at least once a week, that is even better.

Spending time visualizing in the evening just before bed is probably the most powerful. It's been scientifically proven that the thoughts and images that are present in your mind during the last 45 minutes before going to sleep are most likely to replay themselves repeatedly in your subconscious mind while sleeping. Don't be surprised if you find yourself dreaming about the things on your Life Vision Board.

Also, don't be surprised if new opportunities, resources, or unusual coincidences begin to happen in your life. The time you spend meditating on your life purpose will cause things to supernaturally align with your life purpose. And as always, make sure you are journaling the things the Holy Spirit is speaking to you during your meditation times. Write down the dreams you are having that you know are connected. Journal about the things that start to happen. You'll want to remember this time in your life. Someday you'll look back in wonder, knowing that this exercise was used by the Father to reveal the answer to 4th Big Q of life – "Where am I headed?" You will also look back, amazed at how everything on your Life Vision Board came to pass.

CHAPTER EIGHT

The 5th Big Q:
How Do I Get There?

Take small steps every day and one day you will get there.
– Unknown

The last question that we are going to hear from God about together may very well be the most important one. It is one thing to know your divine purpose, but it is another thing altogether to know how to fulfill it. The 5th Big Q: "How do I get there?" is actually a question you don't answer just once. It's a question that you'll need to be asking God on a regular basis. The reason is because the answer to this question is always the same: You'll get to your destiny by following God one step at a time.

When God shows you your purpose and reveals His vision for your life, He shows you the end, not a detailed plan of how to fulfill it. He's like an architect that gives a homebuilder a blueprint of a house to build. A blueprint shows you the big picture, not the process of how to build a house. In the same way, God's vision for your life shows you the big picture of your life. This is why, when you create a vision board, you want it to depict the way your life will look in the future. But answering the 5th Big Q, and knowing how to fulfill your purpose and see your vision come to pass, is a process of hearing from God on a daily basis. It's all about developing intimacy with God.

One of the most frustrating things in the world is to have a vision from God but not to know the first thing about how to go about fulfilling it. Just because you have a prophecy doesn't mean it's automatically going to come to pass. Prophesy, like a vision, requires you to hear from God about how to walk it out on a practical level. Remember, the work God has preordained you to do is supernatural. You are not going to bring the vision for your life to pass on your own. Abraham and Sarah learned this lesson the hard way. When they took matters into their own hands and tried to produce an heir on their own through their servant Hagar, things turned out badly. Both Hagar and Ishmael ended up paying the consequences for their mistake. Yes, Abraham was destined to have a child, but it was going to happen supernaturally, not naturally. There simply is no other way to fulfill God's vision for your life. You are going to have to depend on God to do it.

I can personally attest to the fact that most people who have received a prophetic word or feel like they are clear about their purpose don't see it come to pass. While there are many reasons and excuses people give for not seeing God's promises and visions come to pass in their lives, there is really one thing that holds them back. They lack the intimacy with God that is required for them to follow Him step by step into the fulfillment of His plan for their life. They are not regularly, on a daily basis, hearing from God about their divine purpose. Inevitably, challenges, distractions, or other circumstances arise that cause them to get off track. But, instead of hearing from God in the midst of the situation, they end up using it as an excuse for why they aren't seeing the supernatural fulfillment of what God has spoken to them. On occasion, some people even end up blaming God, believing He is holding something back from them or causing the delay. If you are going to see your divine purpose fulfilled and live the life you are destined by God to live, you are going to have to cultivate the same kind of relationship with Him that Jesus had with the Father.

One Thing Is Needed

Developing the same kind of relationship that Jesus had with the Father may sound like a tall order, but anything less is robbing you of the very thing Jesus came to provide you. Let's look at Matthew 11:27 in the Message Translation again. This is the scripture where Jesus promised to help you develop the same kind of intimate relationship He enjoyed with the Father. Let's dive a bit deeper and look at how Jesus described how important His relationship with the Father was in fulfilling His purpose and divine destiny.

> *Jesus resumed talking to the people, but now tenderly. "The Father has given me all these things to do and say. This is a unique Father-Son operation, coming out of Father and Son intimacies and knowledge. No one knows the Son the way the Father does, nor the Father the way the Son does. But I'm not keeping it to Myself; I'm ready to go over it line by line with anyone willing to listen."*
> – Matthew 11:27 (MSG)

Here Jesus describes His life purpose, saying how the Father has given Him things to do and say. He describes it as a "unique Father-Son operation" that is "coming out of Father and Son intimacies and knowledge." This is extremely insightful. Just like Jesus', your life purpose and divine destiny is also a unique "Father-Son operation." It involves the good or supernatural works that the Father predestined for you to do. The Father has also given you specific things to do and say. The term "Father-Son operation" invokes the idea that this is a partnership between Jesus and the Father. They are working side by side, or in this case inside each other as one, to accomplish the reason Jesus was on the planet. It was the intimacy between the Father and Son that made it possible for Jesus to fulfill his destiny and go to the cross.

Jesus depended completely on the Father to accomplish His divine purpose and fulfill His destiny. He wasn't trying to heal the sick or raise the dead or even go to the cross in His own strength. He was empowered by the Father within Him. The Father in Jesus was doing the work through Jesus. If you are like most people, even Christians, this is an entirely new way of living your life. We are taught to be independent and take care of ourselves. We celebrate the concept of a "self-made" man and tend to view the concept of self-care as being responsible. But, in the kingdom, we are called to live like children.

And he said: "Truly I tell you, unless you change and become like little children,
you will never enter the kingdom of heaven."
– Matthew 18:3 (NIV)

Children don't run the show in a family – at least not in a healthy one, anyway – the parents do. Parents are responsible for caring for the needs of their children and making sure they get where they need to go. Parents drive their kids to school, to soccer practice, and anywhere else they deem appropriate. In the same way, the Father is responsible for your needs and for making sure you get to your destination. In the kingdom, we are called to live dependently, not independently. We, like Jesus, must learn to completely depend on the Father. Jesus' relationship shows us what's possible in our relationship with the Father. The way He lived, in intimate communion with the Father, is now how we can live. All that's needed is desire.

Getting on God's Agenda

In John 5:19–20 and also in verse 30, Jesus says more about how the unique Father-Son operation He was involved in with the Father worked. He paints a picture of what dependency on the Father actually looks like. Jesus was *completely* dependent on the Father. When I say *completely*, I mean 100% of the time – 100% of Jesus' will, 100% of Jesus' emotions, 100% of Jesus' thoughts – 100% of Jesus' entire being was submitted to the Father. Jesus had no agenda of His own. He was completely dependent upon the Father for step-by-step instructions. The Voice Translation of this scripture goes as far as to say Jesus was mimicking the Father.

The truth is that the Son does nothing on His own; all these actions are
led by the Father. The Son watches the Father closely and then mimics
the work of the Father. The Father loves the Son, so He does not hide His
actions. Instead, He shows Him everything, and the things not yet revealed
by the Father will dumbfound you.
– John 5:19–20 (Voice)

I have not ever acted, and will not in the future act, on My own. I listen to the directions of the One who sent Me and act on these divine instructions. For this reason, My judgment is always fair and never self-serving. I'm committed to pursuing God's agenda and not My own.
– John 5:30 (Voice)

In verse 30, it says Jesus never once acted on His own. He simply followed the Father's directions. He didn't have any agenda except the Father's. These scriptures are so powerful. I mean, Jesus Christ, the Son of God, said, "I can do nothing on My own!"

When we read scriptures like these and think about what is required of us to live this way, I think a lot of times our first response is, "I don't know how to do this." We've lived so independently from God for so long, it doesn't occur to us to live any differently. But honestly, it is not complicated. This is so simple, a child can do it. This is what Jesus meant when He told us we were going to have to become like little children to enter the kingdom. I like to think that following the Father is like playing the game "Simon Says." I was at my youngest daughter's school party once and they played "Simon Says." It had been a long time since I had thought about that game. But it was hilarious to watch these kids. They were standing on one foot, raising their arms, and doing all kinds of silly motions. But if they did something Simon didn't say, they had to sit down. I could not help but think of how this was like Jesus mimicking the Father.

Learning to follow directions is part of being a child. Becoming a mature follower of Jesus actually looks like dependence, not independence. The kingdom is completely opposite from the world. As you grow up in Christ, you actually become more dependent on Him. However, following the Father's directions step by step, even though I'm telling you it is simple – because it is – is very uncommon. Most of us are fiercely independent. But abiding in union with God and learning how to fully depend on Him is the most important lesson you need to learn in order to fulfill your life purpose. It puts the only key you'll ever need to reach your destiny in the ignition so you can get started on your way to where you are headed. If you practice union and depend on God on a daily basis, you will reach your destiny – guaranteed.

The Battle for Intimacy

Every battle we face is first and foremost a battle for intimacy with God.
– Graham Cooke

Let this quote from Graham Cooke sink in for a moment. It is spot on. In reality, the battles you encounter as you pursue the call of God on your life and walk out your divine destiny are never really about whatever seemingly impossible circumstance or proverbial giant you are facing. They are always about the strength of your relational connection with God and your identity in Him. The battle is always to keep hearing God's voice. If you live independently, as though the illusion of separation from God is real, you will have a hard time hearing from God when you need it the most. As a result, you will lose sight of your true identity and get off the path that leads to your destiny. There's only one way to get to where you're headed. Reaching your divine destiny is a supernatural journey that God leads you on. You have to hear His instructions and follow them, step by step. If you live disconnected from Him, you'll never reach your destination.

This is why Jesus was so adamant about His "oneness" relationship with the Father. He was constantly pointing people back to it. His union with the Father was at the very core and formed the foundation of His identity. The gospel He preached was "good news" because He was the "way" to our union with the Father. The way He lived as one with the Father demonstrated what being a Son of God was actually supposed to be like. He did not rely on Himself or follow His own agenda. He aligned His will with the Father's agenda and followed His instructions all the way to the cross. Jesus' oneness with the Father is the reason Jesus fulfilled His earthly mission. It will also be the reason you fulfill yours.

When you catch the union message of Jesus and begin to view the gospel and scripture through the lens of "oneness with the Godhead," everything begins to shift. You catch wind of the point of life and connect with the ultimate reason Jesus put on a human suit and experienced human death – your death. It was so you could live inside of God with God living inside of you. If this doesn't revolutionize your life, you might want to check your pulse. Your union with God changes everything. When you begin to really understand this, you morph into someone who lives the same way Jesus did. Said another way, you live a transfigured life, where the Jesus in you begins to be recognized and released through you.

Your union with God is the only equipment you need on your journey to fulfill your divine destiny. Through Christ, you can do all things! You will make supernatural progress toward your divine destiny as you depend fully on the Leader who lives inside of you. Day by day, as you grow in your knowledge of Him and learn to follow Him step by step, you'll find yourself doing the extraordinary exploits – even greater works than Jesus.

Making the Main Thing the Main Thing

Here are few of my favorite scriptures that talk about the power of knowing God intimately and how that leads to living a miraculous life:

> *...the people that do know their God shall be strong, and do exploits.*
> *– Daniel 11:32 (KJV)*

> *Don't let the wise brag of their wisdom. Don't let heroes brag of their exploits.*
> *Don't let the rich brag of their riches. If you brag, brag of this and this only: That*
> *you understand and know Me.*
> *– Jeremiah 9:23 (MSG)*

> *Jesus explained, "I am the Way, I am the Truth, and I am the Life. No one*
> *comes next to the Father except through union with Me. To know Me is to know*
> *my Father too. And from now on you will realize that you have seen Him and*
> *experienced Him." Philip spoke up, "Lord, show us the Father, and that will be all*
> *that we need!" Jesus replied, "Philip, I've been with you all this time and you still*
> *don't know who I am? How could you ask Me to show you the Father, for anyone*
> *who has looked at Me has seen the Father. Don't you believe that the Father is*
> *living in Me and that I am living in the Father? Even My words are not My own*
> *but come from My Father, for He lives in Me and performs His miracles of power*
> *through Me. Believe that I live as one with My Father and that My Father lives as*
> *one with Me – or at least, believe because of the mighty miracles I have done. I*
> *tell you this timeless truth: The person who follows Me in faith, believing in Me,*

will do the same mighty miracles that I do — even greater miracles than these because I go to be with My Father!"
– John 14:6–12 (TPT)

So Jesus said, "I speak to you timeless truth. I never act independently of the Father or do anything through My own initiative. I only do the works that I see the Father doing, for the Son does the same works as His Father. Because the Father loves His Son so much, He always reveals to Me everything that He is about to do. And you will all be amazed when He shows Me even greater works than what you've seen so far! For just like the Father has power to raise the dead, the Son will raise the dead and give them back their life."
– John 5:19–21 (TPT)

Jesus said to them, "Truly, truly, I say to you, the Son can do nothing of His own accord, but only what He sees the Father doing; for whatever He does, that the Son does likewise. For the Father loves the Son, and shows Him all that He Himself is doing; and greater works than these will He show Him, that you may marvel."
– John 5:18–20 (RSV)

I have shown the world Your glory by faithfully doing everything You've told me to do.
– John 17:4 (TPT)

Jesus resumed talking to the people, but now tenderly. "The Father has given Me all these things to do and say. This is a unique Father-Son operation, coming out of Father and Son intimacies and knowledge. No one knows the Son the way the Father does, nor the Father the way the Son does. But I'm not keeping it to Myself; I'm ready to go over it line by line with anyone willing to listen."
– Matthew 11:27 (MSG)

Each one of these scriptures is incredibly powerful. They show how it's not the strong, the brilliant, or the rich who see the impossible and fulfill their divine destinies. It is those who know God intimately. If you want to fulfill your destiny, get to know the Leader that lives within you, and learn to follow His instructions step by step. As you do, you will miraculously fulfill your divine destiny. You will experience the power of the Holy Spirit that dwells within you – the very same Spirit that raised Jesus from the grave. You will do exploits, see greater miracles than you've ever imagined, and be infused with the inner strength you need to overcome anything and everything that the enemy throws at you. Your life, like Jesus', will glorify God and release heaven on earth.

Captivated by Love

God's unconditional love is captivating. The more we experience it, the more we want to experience it and the more we realize our need to experience it. Encounters with God's love become a necessity you simply can't live without. Getting to know God more and more becomes your greatest quest in life. The Apostle Paul's life is a wonderful example of this dichotomy.

Check out this amazing scripture from the Apostle Paul that describes his desire to know God.

> *[For my determined purpose is] that I may know Him [that I may progressively become more deeply and intimately acquainted with Him, perceiving and recognizing and understanding the wonders of His Person more strongly and more clearly], and that I may in that same way come to know the power outflowing from His resurrection [which it exerts over believers], and that I may so share His sufferings as to be continually transformed [in spirit into His likeness even] to His death, [in the hope] That if possible I may attain to the [spiritual and moral] resurrection [that lifts me] out from among the dead [even while in the body]. Not that I have now attained [this ideal], or have already been made perfect, but I press on to lay hold of (grasp) and make my own, that for which Christ Jesus (the Messiah) has laid hold of me and made me His own.*
> *– Philippians 3:10–12 (AMPC)*

I especially love the Amplified translation of this scripture. It amplifies so many things that are worth amplifying. The very first amplification, "for my determined purpose is," points out the process that Paul must have gone through to determine his ultimate purpose. His process, or life journey, brought him to the place where knowing Jesus and experiencing the power of His resurrection was his ultimate pursuit.

The more Paul got to know and experience Jesus, the more he wanted to know and experience. The Apostle Paul didn't know Jesus during Jesus' earthly life. He was introduced to Him, quite dramatically actually, on the road to Damascus. But, eventually, he became a man obsessed with knowing Jesus. As a result, he wrote two-thirds of the New Testament and explained the mystery of the gospel message as union with God through Christ. Paul made it his determined purpose to know what it meant to be "crucified with Christ" (Galatians 2:2) and "resurrected with Christ" (Colossians 3:1). In the Passion Translation of this passage, starting in verse 9, it says Paul's passion was to be consumed with Jesus.

> *My passion is to be consumed with Him and not cling to my own "righteousness" based in keeping the written Law. My "righteousness" will be His, based on the faith of Jesus Christ — the very righteousness of God. And by His faith, I will fully experience oneness with Jesus and the explosive power of his resurrection working in me. I will be one with Him in His sufferings and I will be one with Him in His death. Only then will I be able to experience complete oneness with Him in His resurrection from the realm of death. I admit that I haven't yet acquired the absolute fullness that I'm pursuing, but I run with passion into His abundance so that I may reach the destiny that Jesus Christ has called me to fulfill and wants me to discover.*
> – Philippians 3:9–12 (TPT)

Paul was a man on a mission to experience oneness with Jesus and the power of Jesus' resurrection personally. He was fully aware that this was the path to his destiny. Paul recognized that he would only reach his destiny to the extent he passionately pursued the fullness of his union with Christ.

Paul's revelation is so incredibly powerful and true. My own life bears witness to it. In the process of getting to know God and experiencing our union with Him, we supernaturally fulfill our destiny step by step.

Building Your Confidence

One of the biggest challenges that comes with learning to hear from God is having the confidence to believe we are hearing God correctly and stepping out in faith, especially if what He is telling us to do doesn't make sense or carries some kind of risk. Here are a few practical steps you can take to build your confidence and help you hear God more clearly on a consistent basis.

1. Practice

We don't do anything perfectly the first time we attempt it. The old adage "Practice makes perfect" is definitely true. If you really want to jump-start your ability to hear God, make journaling a daily practice. I know a lot of people resist this. They believe they aren't the "journaling type," whatever that means. But unless you have a physical disability of some kind that hinders you from picking up a pen, opening your journal, and writing, this belief is hindering your spiritual progress and delaying you on your journey to get to where you are headed.

In Matthew 6:11, Jesus instructed his disciples to ask the Father for "daily bread." While this might apply to asking for food that nourishes us physically on a daily basis, it also definitely applies to asking for spiritual nourishment. The Father has "daily bread" for you to eat that will strengthen you spiritually. He has daily instructions, guidance, and wisdom to give you. He wants to help you live an abundant life and experience heaven on earth, every single day.

Unfortunately, daily journaling is not something most people practice. This is also one of the reasons so many are wandering in the wilderness, never reaching their promised lands. There is something powerful that happens when we place a value on God's words on a daily basis.

> *Blessed are those who listen to Me, watching daily at My doors,*
> *waiting at My doorway.*
> – Proverbs 8:34 NIV

2. Make Space to Hear God

All of us are busy. The idea of adding one more thing to your calendar may feel like you are going into "tilt" mode. However, until we come to the place where hearing from God is our number one priority, we will waste time. No matter how busy you are, taking time to listen to the voice of God, even for a few minutes, will help you gain focus for the rest of your day. It will actually save you time. Hearing God helps you prioritize everything else. Remember, walking in union with God means letting go of your agenda and getting onto His. God is more concerned about your schedule than you are. He knows the limitations of your schedule. But he also knows how to maximize your potential and produce supernatural results. Making space on your daily schedule to journal and practice hearing from God is the best way to invest your time. Time spent with God is never wasted time.

3. Don't Do All the Talking

Listen more than you talk when you have a conversation with God. Ask questions rather than make requests. Let God lead the conversation. When He tells you something, ask Him to elaborate. Take copious notes. You are having a meeting with the Creator of the Universe. The Holy Spirit is a genius. So, take time to listen. You learn best by listening, not talking. Practice reflective listening, where you repeat back to God what you are hearing in your own words to make sure you understand what He's speaking.

Developing intimacy with God, practicing union with Jesus, and learning to abide in the Vine (John 15:4) changes your life forever. It will lead you into a lifestyle of hearing God moment by moment. And, although it takes time and practice to hear clearly and consistently, there's no better investment you can make in your future. Hearing is the first step of following. If you are going to follow the Leader to get where you are headed, you're going to have to develop a lifestyle of hearing Him moment by moment.

Practicing the Presence

In the end, the answer to the 5th Big Q, "How do I get there?" is very simple. The way that you get to where you're going is by abiding in Christ as a lifestyle. It is remembering you are one with God in Christ. Jesus, who is one with the Father and the Holy Spirit, lives inside of you and you live inside of Him. Fulfilling your destiny is about remembering who you really are and living out of this reality. It's communing with God in the moment, as a way of life. Truthfully, this moment is all you really own anyway. The past is gone and the future is yet to be. The only moment you have to abide in Christ is this one. And when you reach the next moment, you can then choose to abide in Christ then.

Practicing the presence of God is another term for abiding in Christ. It was made popular by a 17th-century monk named Brother Lawrence. Practicing the presence of God is simply the practice of staying aware of God with you and in you. It is the continual remembrance that you are not alone. I like to think of it as "staying awake" to the indwelling presence of God and the reality of the spiritual realm. It is a state of being where you are using your spiritual senses as well as your physical senses. This is actually supposed to be the normal state for those who confess Christ. It is also another way to think about what the Bible refers to as "walking in the Spirit" (Galatians 5:16) and "being led by the Spirit" (Romans 8:14). As believers, we are called to grow up so that we are like Christ, conformed to His image.

No! We will speak the truth with love. We will grow up in every way to be like Christ, who is the head.
– Ephesians 4:15 (ICB)

For those God foreknew he also predestined to be conformed to the image of his Son, that he might be the firstborn among many brothers and sisters.
– Romans 8:29 (NIV)

To grow up to be just like Jesus means that you have the exact kind of relationship He enjoyed with the Father and as a result, you fulfill the Father's purpose and destiny for your life the same way Jesus did. You live as one with the Father, abiding in Christ. As you do this, at the end of your life, you'll be able to say the same thing Jesus said at the end of His.

I glorified you on earth by completing down to the last detail what you assigned me to do.
– John 17:4 (MSG)

Love Letter from God

My Incredible Child,

I am so happy that you decided to embark on this journey with Me to answer The 5 Big Qs of Life. The adventure we have begun together is just beginning. Every step we take toward the fulfillment of your purpose and the way to your destiny is meant to teach you something very important. There are lessons that you will learn about yourself, about just how glorious I created you to be. You are going to learn to break through the limitations of the natural realm and allow Me to do the impossible through you. You are also going to learn how to see things completely differently, from My perspective, as we sit together on My throne in heaven.

But I think the lessons I am most excited to teach you are the ones that reveal My heart to you. Telling you I am unbelievably good and you experiencing My almost-too-good-to-be-true goodness are two very different things. I am going to astound you with My goodness and make you a trophy of My grace. I want others to be able to recognize the kind of Father I am through your life. I want people to look at your life and know that I love extravagantly and give freely out of the abundance of My inexhaustible grace and riches. I share My life and reveal My goodness to everyone who sincerely seeks Me. And you, My child, are going to be a living example of this.

I completely understand how you are still learning to trust Me and that's okay. I have patience for miles. You can walk as slowly or run as swiftly as you want down My path of life. I am not in a hurry, Me just being with you always is what's most important to Me.

Kisses from Heaven,
Dad

Digging Deeper Exercise 1 – Practicing God's Presence

Can I bring the Lord back into my mind-flow every few seconds so that God shall always be in my mind? I choose to make the rest of my life an experiment in answering this question.
– Frank Laubach

For this first exercise, we are going to practice abiding in Christ and practicing the presence of God. Remember, the goal is to maintain a conscious awareness of the indwelling presence of Jesus, the Father, and the Holy Spirit and to awake to the realm of the Spirit. As you work through the exercise, engage all five of your spiritual senses, becoming aware of what you see, hear, feel, smell, and taste.

STEP 1 – Meditation

Spend 10–15 minutes, on a daily basis as needed, speaking the following truths over yourself until they become a part of your consciousness and thought life.

- Jesus, the Father, and the Holy Spirit are always present with me, living within me, whether I am aware of it or not.
- Jesus, the Father, and the Holy Spirit are always active in my life, whether I sense it or not.
- Learning to recognize and experience the presence of Jesus, the Father, and the Holy Spirit is a learned behavior that I can cultivate and grow in.
- My determined purpose is to be aware of Jesus, the Father, and the Holy Spirit in the present moment, moment by moment, and to experience my union with Him.
- I am in Christ. I am _____ (insert your name) wearing a Jesus suit.
- Christ is in me. Jesus is wearing a _____ (insert your name) suit.
- I am never separated from Jesus, the Father, and the Holy Spirit, even when I make mistakes or fall short of His glory and sin. Whenever I

feel separated from God and lose my sense of God's presence, I will simply recognize the feeling as a feeling and then release the illusion of separation to God while visualizing Jesus living inside me.

- Whenever I fail to remember God's presence, I can always start again right away.
- My desire for God may ebb and flow, but His desire for me is constant.
- Every thought and feeling I experience moves me a little closer to or a little farther from an awareness of God's presence. Therefore, I will stay aware of my inner world and if needed, stop throughout the day to remember who I really am and visualize my union with God in Christ.
- Every aspect of my life – work, relationships, hobbies, errands, etc. – is of immense and genuine interest to God. He enjoys being involved in the details of my life.
- Straining and trying to abide are pointless and do not help. Resting and trusting in what Jesus has already accomplished is all that is required.

As you wrap up your meditation time, take a few moments to visualize your union with God in Christ. As we learned previously, "put on Christ" (Galatians 3:27). Visualize yourself wearing a "Jesus suit." Alternatively, visualize Christ in you. See Jesus wearing a "you" suit.

STEP 2 – Staying in the Now

After meditating on the truths in step 1 and visualizing your union with God through Jesus, the next step is to practice staying in this place of union throughout the day and living in the present moment. For this exercise, you are going to need a timer. Most smartphones these days give you the ability to set a timer using reminders or an alarm. If you don't have a smartphone, you may want to use a cooking timer. The goal, of course, is to stay aware of God's presence and your union with Him moment by moment. However, setting an alarm at intervals throughout the day as a reminder to practice God's presence will help you stay on track.

- Using a timer, set an alarm for every hour you will be awake.

- Throughout the day, try to live in the present moment, aware of your union with Christ.
- Remember, there is literally no way to practice God's presence if you are being pulled into the past (via shame, regret, etc.) or into the future (via worry).
- When an alarm goes off, ask yourself, how aware of God was I in this last hour?
- If I was pulled off track, what caused it?
- After a few moments of reflection, read through the list of truths from step 1 if needed.
- After reading through the list, once again tune your awareness to your union with Christ.
- Continue practicing the presence of God for the remainder of the day, repeating the process as needed.

STEP 3 - Journal

At the end of the day, before heading to bed, take a few minutes to journal about your experience that day practicing the presence of God and abiding in Christ.

- How did it go?
- Was it difficult to stay focused?
- What pulled you off track the most?
- Did you notice yourself living in the moment, thinking about the past, or worrying?

Digging Deeper Exercise 2 - Hearing Specific Instructions

For this next exercise, you are going to practice asking and receiving specific instructions from God. The goal is to let the Holy Spirit lead the conversation. Therefore, it is important to approach this exercise with an open mind. Before beginning, you'll want to set aside 30–60 minutes of uninterrupted time on your calendar. It may not take that long, but it's always best to leave yourself some leeway.

STEP 1 - Set the Atmosphere

Before beginning, you will want to set the atmosphere:

- Set aside a few moments to get yourself in the right frame of mind.
- The goal is to clear your mind of distractions and connect with your spirit.
- Consider having soft, worshipful music playing in the background or lighting a candle.
- Once you feel connected and can sense God's presence, you're ready to move to the next step.

STEP 2 - Pray

Pray the following prayer out loud.

Holy Spirit, Thank you for joining me today and helping me grow in my ability to hear from and depend on You. Open my ears and teach me to really listen to what You have to say and receive specific instructions from You. I yield myself to You completely and release whatever might be on my heart to You. I want to follow Your agenda, not mine. If there are burdens that I am carrying, even unaware, I ask You to help me release them to You now (Take a few moments to release to Jesus whatever cares, concerns, and burdens you have). Thank You for being a patient teacher and for helping me learn how to abide in the Vine, follow Your lead, and walk in the Spirit. In Jesus' name, AMEN!

STEP 3 - Journal

Starting with a new page in your journal, ask the Holy Spirit who would like to speak with you today – Himself, the Father, or Jesus. Once you hear the answer, ask the following questions to whichever member of the Trinity the Holy Spirit said you'd be hearing from today. Write down whatever you hear in your journal.

- What would You like to speak to me today?
- *Why do I need to know this?*
- What specific instructions would You like to give me today?
- Is there anything else I should ask You?
- Ask the additional questions.

STEP 4 - Follow the Leader

Starting with a new page in your journal, write down the instructions God gave you. Afterward, ask the Holy Spirit the following questions and write down whatever you hear in your journal:

- How should I go about carrying out the instructions I received?
- Is this something that I should do today? If not, when?
- What else do I need to know?
- If you have concerns, fears, or additional questions, take time to journal about these.
- Once you have clarity, follow the instructions you received and do whatever God asks you to do.

Before going to bed, write down what happened as a result of following God's instructions.

- How did it feel to follow the instructions God gave you?
- Did things work as planned?
- Was it clear afterward that you heard God correctly?
- If not, what happened? What can you learn from this experience?

CHAPTER NINE

Dealing with Detours, Breakdowns, and Roadblocks

The greater the obstacle, the more glory in overcoming it.
— Molière

As you head down The Path and pursue your life purpose and the fulfillment of the vision God has for your life, I will go ahead and warn you right now, you are going to run into roadblocks, breakdowns, and detours. There are going to be days that you feel like throwing in the towel. You are going to encounter opposition along the way. It is simply inevitable. There's not a single person who has made a difference in the world who didn't have to "overcome the odds," experience failure, or be tempted at least once to say, "Forget it, this is too hard. I can't do it."

It is a fairytale to think that pursuing a life worth living is easy or that it will not require you to grow and face your deepest fears. Not everyone is going to agree with the decisions you make or encourage you to keep going when it feels like everything is falling apart. Leaving the status quo and pushing through limitations that other people think are impossible upsets some people. Rejection is almost guaranteed. And remember, your purpose is, by design, something you won't do alone. It is going to require dependency on and faith in God. Reaching your destiny involves the supernatural!

If it makes you feel any better, even Jesus wasn't popular with everyone. His life was a threat to the religious and political systems of His day. The pressure on Him to quit before being arrested and going to the cross was so intense, He started sweating drops of blood.

> *And being in agony, He prayed more earnestly; and His sweat became like great drops of blood falling down to the ground.*
> *– Luke 22:44 (WEB)*

Sweating blood, by the way, is a real physical condition. It's called hematidrosis. It is caused when the capillary blood vessels that feed the sweat glands rupture and it only occurs when someone is under extreme physical or emotional stress. While I am not saying that pursuing your life purpose will bring you to this point of duress, I am saying that you shouldn't just expect to waltz into your destiny. Life in the Kingdom of God, this side of heaven, is not trouble-free. We were never promised that following Jesus would be without trials or tribulation. What we are promised is that, through Christ, we can endure and overcome whatever life throws our way, because He has already overcome it all.

> *And everything I've taught you is so that the peace which is in Me will be in you and will give you great confidence as you rest in Me. For in this unbelieving world, you will experience trouble and sorrows, but you must be courageous, for I have conquered the world!*
> *– John 16:33 (TPT)*

> *By nature, in Christ, you are an overcomer. You are **more** than a conqueror. I have told you these things, so that in Me you may have peace. In this world you will have trouble. But take heart! I have overcome the world.*
> *– John 16:33 (NIV)*

> *Yet in all these things we are more than conquerors through Him who loved us.*
> *– Romans 8:37 (NKJV)*

Facing the Giants

Releasing your full potential, by its very nature, requires that you break through the things that have kept your potential bottled up and obscured from view. It also requires that you trust God to lead you step by step into doing things that in your own ability and strength you would never be able to accomplish. I oftentimes liken us reaching our destiny to the story of the Israelites possessing the Promised Land. There are so many wonderful lessons to learn from their experiences. If you are familiar with the story, you know the Israelites escaped slavery under Pharaoh in Egypt by following Moses into the wilderness. There is a crucial point in the story, however, when they reach the edge of the Promised Land and send in spies to scope out the current inhabitants who are living there.

Now they departed and came back to Moses and Aaron and all the congregation of the children of Israel in the Wilderness of Paran, at Kadesh; they brought back word to them and to all the congregation, and showed them the fruit of the land. Then they told him, and said: "We went to the land where you sent us. It truly flows with milk and honey, and this is its fruit. Nevertheless the people who dwell in the land are strong; the cities are fortified and very large; moreover we saw the descendants of Anak there. The Amalekites dwell in the land of the South; the Hittites, the Jebusites, and the Amorites dwell in the mountains; and the Canaanites dwell by the sea and along the banks of the Jordan." Then Caleb quieted the people before Moses, and said, "Let us go up at once and take possession, for we are well able to overcome it." But the men who had gone up with him said, "We are not able to go up against the people, for they are stronger than we." And they gave the children of Israel a bad report of the land which they had spied out, saying, "The land through which we have gone as spies is a land that devours its inhabitants, and all the people whom we saw in it are men of great stature. There we saw the giants (the descendants of Anak came from the giants); and we were like grasshoppers in our own sight, and so we were in their sight."
– Numbers 13:26–33 (NKJV)

Here at this critical point in the story, we find two kinds of people – people who overcome the odds to fulfill their divine destiny and people who quit along the way. After the spies reported there were giants in the land, one of the spies, named Caleb, stepped up with confidence, saying, "Let us go up at once and take possession, for we are well able to overcome it." But the other spies weren't so sure. In verse 33, it says they saw themselves like grasshoppers compared to the giants. They even went so far as to say that the giants also saw them that way.

Ultimately, if you know the story, they never made it into the Promised Land. Instead, the unbelieving Israelites died in the wilderness after wandering aimlessly for 40 years. But it wasn't the giants' fault. It was their own self-image that prohibited them from experiencing what God had promised to them. Because they saw themselves as grasshoppers, they literally couldn't believe God's promise, prophecy, and destiny for their lives. But it wasn't just what they believed about themselves that held them back. What they believed about God also played a part. They didn't trust God to do the impossible through them. I call this the "grasshopper syndrome."

If you read the entire story, you'll find they kept accusing God of bringing them out of Egypt to kill them. They not only had a distorted image of themselves but also had a distorted image of God. As a result, they limited what was possible for their lives and didn't see the divine destiny God had planned for them come to pass.

In our own lives, as we pursue our own personal Promised Land, we may not have to face physical giants, but we will absolutely all have to deal with the "grasshopper syndrome." We have to confront our own beliefs about ourselves, God, and what is possible. This is why so much of the work I do with clients and my Emerge students is focused on supernatural mind renewal. Helping people to connect with God – to supernaturally transform the self-limiting, subconscious beliefs about themselves, God, and what is possible for their lives – is at the very core of everything I do.

One of the most life-transforming parts of Emerge is the Rethink Rapid Mind Renewal (RMR) sessions that students participate in twice a month. You don't have to be enrolled in Emerge to do Rethink RMR sessions. People from all over the country actually do them on a regular basis as well. A Rethink RMR session is a two-hour facilitated conversation with God that helps you uncover memories and negative beliefs, both conscious and subconscious, that are hindering you from releasing your full potential in Christ or that are causing you pain or limiting you in any way. Once these areas are uncovered, we use different tools and communication with God to bring you to a new place of peace, wholeness, and freedom. It is incredible the things that God is doing in these sessions.

Dealing with Detours

The Israelites, because of their inability to see themselves and God correctly, went on a 40-year *detour* into the wilderness. While they were on this incredibly long detour, although they were supernaturally sustained by God, many of them died never having the opportunity to experience the life God had planned for them.

I have led you forty years in the desert. Your clothes did not wear out. And your shoes did not wear out on your feet. You did not eat bread, or drink wine or strong drink, so you might know that I am the Lord your God.
– Deuteronomy 29:5–6 (NLV)

Because we are all growing and renewing our minds as to who we are in Christ, and learning to trust God by getting to know God for who He really is, most of us at some point will end up taking one or more unplanned detours on the way to our destiny. Detours can show up as opportunities, challenges, or really anything that you encounter that causes a delay or for you to seemingly wander, making no real forward progress.

In my own life, I've definitely experienced detours on the way to fulfilling my life purpose. One in particular lasted five years. It was a painful but enlightening season of learning to embrace who God created me to be and overcome the opinions of others. Interestingly, God actually warned me before I headed into the detour. But honestly, because of my subconscious fears and wrong self-image, I didn't really understand what was happening at first. But, thankfully, by the grace of God, I was able to recognize that I was headed down the wrong road and needed to go back on the path to becoming who God had created me to be. I was able to lay aside the opinions of other people and what they thought I should be and do and fully embrace the call of God on my life.

Even Jesus was tested in the area of His identity. He headed into the wilderness for 40 days and had His identity and self-concept tested big time. It was right after His baptism when the Father verbally confirmed who Jesus was, His beloved Son, and the Holy Spirit descended upon Him.

And as Jesus rose up out of the water, the heavenly realm opened up over Him and he saw the Holy Spirit descend out of the heavens and rest upon Him in the form of a dove. Then suddenly the voice of the Father shouted from the sky, saying, "This is the Son I love, and My greatest delight is in Him."
– Matthew 3:16–17 (TPT)

In Matthew 4 is where things get interesting.

Afterward, the Holy Spirit led Jesus into the lonely wilderness in order to reveal His strength against the accuser by going through the ordeal of testing. And after fasting for forty days, Jesus was extremely weak and famished. Then the tempter came to entice Him to provide food by doing a miracle. So he said to Jesus, "How can you possibly be the Son of God and go hungry? Just order these stones to be turned into loaves of bread." He answered, "The Scriptures say: Bread alone will not satisfy, but true life is found in every word which constantly goes forth from God's mouth." Then the accuser transported Jesus to the holy city of Jerusalem and perched Him at the highest point of the temple and said to Him, "If you're really God's Son, jump, and the angels will catch you. For it is written in the Scriptures: He will command His angels to protect you and they will lift you up so that you won't even bruise your foot on a rock." Once again Jesus said to him, "The Scriptures say: You must never put the Lord your God to a test." And the third time, the accuser lifted Jesus up into a very high mountain range and showed Him all the kingdoms of the world and all the splendor that goes with it. "All of these kingdoms I will give to you," the accuser said, "if only you will kneel down before me and worship me." But Jesus said, "Go away, enemy! For the Scriptures say: Kneel before the Lord your God, and worship only Him." At once the accuser left Him, and angels suddenly gathered around Jesus to minister to His needs.
– Mathew 4: 1-11 (TPT)

Over and over again, the enemy tested Jesus' self-concept. "Are you really the Son of God? If so, prove it!" However, Jesus responded every time from

His true identity. He didn't suffer from the "grasshopper syndrome." He knew who He was and who His Father was. As a result, the detour lasted only 40 days instead of 40 years.

When you find yourself faced with a detour on the way to your destiny, like me, you may not realize what is happening at first. However, circumstances have a way of revealing what is in our hearts. If you find yourself doubting your life purpose, getting offended with God, or struggling with low self-esteem, chances are you are in the middle of a detour. You aren't making progress toward your destiny; you might even be headed in the wrong direction.

The first thing to do when you find yourself in this predicament is to realize what's happening. You can't correct a problem you don't realize you have. I realize that "waking up" to what's really going on isn't always easy. That's why it's so important to have the right mentors and other relationships in your life. I call these people your "soul tribe." You are not designed to "go it alone."

Who you spend time with is who you will emulate. You will absolutely embody the traits and expectations of your peer group. The environment you cultivate will be the environment that molds you.

Walk with the wise and become wise; associate with fools and get in trouble.
– Proverbs 13:20 (NLT)

If you surround yourself with negativity and people who are suffering with the "grasshopper syndrome," you will end up taking unnecessary detours and possibly even miss your destiny. But, if you surround yourself with "overcomers," people who have overcome the things you are facing and have experienced what is required to possess the Promised Land, they can help you get back on track and stay encouraged.

It is always easier for others, especially those who have gone through the things you may be experiencing, to see your "blind spots" and help you identify what's really going on in your life. If you aren't connected with a mentor and people you know are your soul tribe, or you feel you need more support, consider becoming a part of Emerge. Emerge is an incredible community of people who are called to make a difference and who are serious about confronting and overcoming whatever they need to in order to fulfill their destiny. Emerge gives you the tools – like the Rethink RMR sessions – and the support you need to deal with detours and whatever self-limiting beliefs might be holding you back.

Dealing with Breakdowns

Breakdowns, like detours, are usually inevitable as you travel down the path to your destiny. But, unlike detours that cause you to head in the wrong direction, breakdowns cause you to get completely stuck. You aren't going anywhere and your life pretty much ends up looking the same year after year. Sometimes the breakdowns occur because of a negative self-image. Other times they occur because of a negative habit or behavior that keeps you stuck. And at other times, they occur because you won't take personal responsibility for where you are in life. You are playing the blame game and blaming yourself, blaming God, or blaming others for your lot in life. Regardless of what causes the breakdown, until you get to the heart of the matter, you will remain stuck.

Take Kyle, one of my executive coaching clients who was also an Emerger. When I met Kyle, he was a successful CEO who had made millions in business. But he had also lost millions. For several years his business hadn't been doing well. As a result, his family had lost everything. Things were beginning to turn around, but he wasn't able to fully take advantage of the opportunities in front of him. Something was holding him back. He couldn't place his finger on it, but he was filled with anxiety about his situation. He found himself thinking negatively all the time. What if things didn't work out again? He had put his family through so much already. Maybe God was trying to teach him something through all of the suffering. Kyle was plagued with doubt and fear.

In Kyle's case, there were a number of "giants" he was going to have to overcome if he was going to fulfill his destiny. He was also smack dab in the middle of a breakdown. If you asked Kyle what he believed his life purpose was, he would answer confidently, "To create wealth for the glory of God and build His kingdom." However, Kyle's past business failures were tainting his future. Subconsciously, Kyle was playing the blame game. He didn't trust God and he blamed Him for not keeping his family from losing everything. But he also wasn't aware of his true feelings. He had grown up in church and felt it was "wrong" to be offended with God. Therefore, he was subconsciously repressing his feelings. It wasn't until his RMR session that his real problem was revealed.

During the session, the Father reconfirmed Kyle's destiny. He also assured him that He had nothing to do with Kyle's business losses. He was a Restorer, not a Destroyer. In fact, if Kyle would remember, He had tried to warn him about the deals that cost him millions. Kyle, not realizing his lack of peace was from God, had moved forward anyway. But, if Kyle would trust Him, He would lead him into new levels of prosperity he had been afraid to receive. As the session continued, the Father revealed the real reason Kyle was stuck. It was a result of him not feeling worthy of money.

Kyle had grown up very poor and his natural father always hated rich people. In fact, he would curse them under his breath whenever he saw them. If someone was driving a luxury car, Kyle's dad would say, "I bet he cheated hundreds of people to get that." During the session, Kyle began to understand why he wasn't able to hold on to the levels of success he achieved in business. As a matter of fact, he saw a pattern of self-sabotaging behavior that had kept him from being successful in sports as a teenager and in other competitions over the years. The bottom line was: Kyle felt guilty for being successful.

By the end of the session, Kyle was a new man. By bringing the subconscious issues to the surface, the Holy Spirit helped Kyle see the lies he had believed that had caused his financial ruin. Kyle left the session excited to share his revelations with his wife and get to work with God as his new business partner.

As you can see from Kyle's experience, if Kyle was going to reach his destiny and fulfill his purpose in life, he was going to have to overcome the breakdown he had suffered in his business. Like most breakdowns, if you want to get back on the road, you are going to have to find the cause of the problem. In Kyle's case, there were several issues. One was related to his image of God and the other was related to his image of himself. Along the path to purpose, even though you have formulated an answer to the 5 Big Qs, you'll always be solidifying your answers, especially to the 1st Big Q, Who is God? and the 2nd Big Q, Who am I? The reason is that there is always more to learn about God and yourself. Also, the different circumstances we face along the way to fulfilling our purpose have a way of bringing up the subconscious beliefs that are really driving our behavior.

But, thankfully, you don't have to go it alone. Like Kyle, if you find yourself stuck on the side of the road on the path to purpose, help is on the way. You can always link up with Emerge and schedule a Rethink RMR session to uncover the cause of your breakdown.

If you are interested in scheduling a Rethink RMR session or finding out more about these life-transforming sessions, you can email us at transformation@ schlyce.com. The sessions are led by our team of certified facilitators who are seasoned in using methodologies that are centered on the presence of God and conversational prayer, yet grounded in neuroscience. Sessions are offered in person, online, and over the phone.

Dealing with Roadblocks

One of the biggest obstacles, if not the biggest obstacle, you will face on the way to your destiny are roadblocks. I haven't met a person yet who didn't encounter at least one roadblock in the process of possessing their Promised Land. Even if you are already extravagantly successful, I can promise you that there may still be a roadblock in your way that is blocking you from achieving your full potential in Christ. In fact, the more successful you get, the more urgent it becomes to identify and overcome roadblocks. Otherwise, the ground you gain will be in jeopardy of being lost. New levels of success will be short-lived.

Roadblocks are upper-limit problems. They are internal, subconscious, set points that keep us from experiencing the fullness of God's kingdom in this life. Because we live in a fallen world, all of us have been programmed, to some extent, to expect the worst. Truth be told, Christians may be some of the worst. We look at the afterlife as being heaven rather than realizing that, through Jesus, heaven has already come to earth. We also, through all kinds of end-times doom-and-gloom eschatology, have been taught that the world is getting darker and darker and will continue to do so until the return of Jesus.

While it is beyond the scope of this book to present an alternative, victorious eschatology, it is important that you recognize how your end-times view of the world affects the future expectations you have for your life. It also affects, to at least some degree, what effect your life can have on the world. If you believe things are going to get worse and worse, what's the point of even trying to make a difference in the world? Honestly, our end-times theology matters more than we may realize.

There is both a present and a future reality to God's kingdom. Embracing the present reality of God's kingdom and the authority of Jesus to make the earth look like heaven here and now may require a huge shift in your perspective, but it is a necessary one. When Jesus said, "Go into all the world and make disciples of nations," it was a call to transform the world (Matthew 28:19). It was a call for you to be a part of heaven's ongoing invasion of the earth that began with Jesus' ministry. Over and over again at the onset of His ministry, Jesus proclaimed the Kingdom of God was at hand (Matthew 3:2, Matthew 4:17, Mark 1:15).

Now, as the body of Christ, you are called to continue the work Jesus began. The Christ in you is the hope of heaven's glory in the earth right now (Colossians 1:27). You are called to do even greater works than Jesus (John 14:12). If all of this sounds too good to be true, welcome to the reality of roadblocks. What you are feeling and sensing is your head crashing into your own upper-limit problem.

You see, everyone, regardless of their theology, has developed, to some degree, a subconscious intolerance to things going too well in our lives for any prolonged length of time. Truth be told, we expect more hell than heaven on earth. Yes, this intolerance stems from our eschatology, but we have a lifetime of negative experiences to back it up. It is actually these negative experiences that develop within us an inability to believe and trust in the extravagant goodness of God. It limits our ability to feel good feelings for any prolonged length of time and hinders our ability to receive increasingly good things in our life.

Honestly, this is why I believe the author of gloom-and-doom eschatology isn't God at all. If I was the enemy who had been stripped of all power and authority (Mathew 28:18, Ephesians 1:21–22, Philippians 2:9) and my only remaining weapon was deception (2 Corinthians 11:3, Ephesians 6:11), I'd try to deceive the church into believing they were powerless to do anything about the future. I would strip them of the authority that Jesus had given them so that I could still rule the world, even though I'd been defeated.

Thankfully, I'm not the enemy, but hopefully you see my point. You are one with God Almighty. Your potential to transform the world into heaven is Christ in you! However, the situation we all have to face, the roadblock in our mind that keeps us from experiencing heaven on earth, in a nutshell is this: The goodness of God is so good it is foreign to us. And although the Bible is chock full of scriptures that speak about the goodness of God, our experiences and our eschatology have taught us otherwise.

> *Give thanks to the LORD, for he is good; his love endures forever.*
> – Psalms 107:1 (NIV)

> *Every good and perfect gift is from above, coming down from the Father of the heavenly lights, who does not change like shifting shadows.*
> – James 1:17 (NIV)

> *Oh, taste and see that the LORD is good! Blessed is the man who takes refuge in him!*
> – Psalms 34:8 (ESV)

> *And we know that in all things God works for the good of those who love Him, who have been called according to His purpose.*
> – Romans 8:28 (NIV)

Although these and many other scriptures teach us that God is incredibly good, the rest of the world doesn't operate the way God does. Not yet anyway. In the "real world," bad things happen to good people every single day. Catastrophes and bad news gain more press than the good things that are happening in the world. Negativity and human suffering are broadcast daily. Heaven has yet to fully occupy earth. As a result, human beings in general have grown accustomed to pain and adversity. We think hell on earth is more normal than heaven on earth and we expect more of the same.

On an individual level, the results of the upper-limit roadblock can be devastating. It has become more "normal" for us to feel fearful than joyful. It's more "natural" to feel bad than good. We fear the future more than we believe we have the God-given power to shape it. We grow up being taught things like, "The only sure things in life are death and taxes," or "Nothing in life is free," or "If it seems too good to be true, then it probably is." And while these ideas might serve us well as we navigate through life in a fallen world, they are considered blasphemy in the kingdom of God.

But until our minds are radically renewed, without even trying, we are suspicious when things start going "too well" for us. We've been taught to expect the proverbial axe to fall whenever things are going well. In fact, we are so accustomed to living a life less than the abundant, heaven-on-earth life God planned for us and we are so unaccustomed to things always going well, we feel extremely uncomfortable, even guilty, when we experience new levels of favor and success. Oftentimes, we will even subconsciously self-sabotage to get our lives back into a place where we feel more comfortable. You simply cannot rise above your own self-image or your own opinion of God's goodness toward you.

The Abnormal Normal

The unfortunate reality is that most people have a limited tolerance for feeling good. If things are going "too well" for "too long" or they feel "too good" for "too long," it feels unnatural, like something is wrong. How much is "too good" and how long is "too long" is relative, of course, and varies from person to person. But overall, it seems that most of us have never developed the ability to let ourselves feel good and have things go well for any significant period of time.

When we hit this roadblock, we hit our upper limit or internal setpoint, and our minds go into tilt mode. It's as though we hit an invisible ceiling on our ability to feel good. We bang our heads against it every time things begin to get "too good" in our lives. As a result, without even realizing it, we turn our attention to something that will cause us to worry or feel fearful or sad so that we can be more comfortable. We manufacture thoughts that bring us back to feeling feelings that are more familiar. For most, this means the negative ones.

But the problem is way bigger than just internal feelings. Most people have a limited tolerance for their lives being extravagantly blessed by God. In fact, it actually frightens us. For example, check out Peter's reaction to Jesus blessing him with an abundance of fish. This story is found in Luke 5:1–11:

One day as Jesus was preaching on the shore of the Sea of Galilee, great crowds pressed in on Him to listen to the word of God. He noticed two empty boats at the water's edge, for the fishermen had left them and were washing their nets. Stepping into one of the boats, Jesus asked Simon, its owner, to push it out into the water. So He sat in the boat and taught the crowds from there. When He had finished speaking, He said to Simon, "Now go out where it is deeper, and let down your nets to catch some fish." "Master," Simon replied, "we worked hard all last night and didn't catch a thing. But if you say so, I'll let the nets down again." And this time their nets were so full of fish they began to tear! A shout for help brought their partners in the other boat, and soon both boats were filled with fish and on the verge of sinking. When Simon Peter realized what had happened, he fell to his knees before Jesus and said, "Oh, Lord, please leave me — I'm such a sinful man." For he was awestruck by the number of fish they had caught, as were the others with him. His partners, James and John, the sons of Zebedee, were also amazed. Jesus replied to Simon, "Don't be afraid! From now on you'll be fishing for people!" And as soon as they landed, they left everything and followed Jesus.

Luke 5:1–11 (NLT)

Isn't Peter's reaction to God's abundance and blessing interesting? What caused him to react this way? His invisible ceiling, of course. However, here's the real issue – we all struggle to believe God is really as good as He claims. We've heard the gospel, we've heard about the goodness of God, we've heard about His kingdom invading the earth, but for some reason, unbeknown to us, we are afraid to receive it.

Deep down inside, we believe we don't deserve God's goodness. We relate to our sinfulness more than our righteousness. As a result, we don't experience the fullness of what it means to be one with God. We don't experience the full reality of our union with Christ. We end up living a life that is conformed to this world rather than one where the Jesus in us is seen through us. We have an invisible ceiling problem. We need to renew our minds!

What's needed is a revelation and a life-changing encounter with the goodness of God! He can shatter the invisible ceiling in an instant. And He must. God's plan for your life is so incredibly good, it is unbelievable in a natural sense. Unless you have experienced heaven, how can it invade earth through you? Unless you've tasted the goodness of God yourself, how can you really believe it's true?

In the kingdom, the Father's goodness is meant to be experienced. The impossible is possible. Unfathomable blessings are expected. Righteous, peace, and joy (good feelings) are normal. As His kingdom expands and increases, things get better and better, not worse. We go from faith to faith and glory to glory. Our future is full of victory, promises are fulfilled, and unspeakable glory is revealed. Now is the time for you to begin experiencing it.

Identifying There's a Roadblock

Most sincere followers of Jesus have yet to experience the reality of His abundant life. Instead, because of the painful things they've experienced in life, they have learned to expect the worst. Their hearts and minds have been programmed to expect pain, and as a result, they are simply better at feeling bad than feeling good. Some of them, you could say, are even experts at feeling bad. They feel bad for others, they feel bad for themselves, they feel bad about others, and they feel bad about themselves. They have grown so accustomed to feeling negative feelings, it's abnormal to feel joyful for too long.

From a neural science perspective, this isn't great news. Over the course of life, most of us have developed millions of nerve connections that are devoted to registering pain. A huge expanse of territory in our hearts is dedicated to feeling fear. Certainly, we have pleasure connections as well, but far too often these pale in comparison with our ability to process pain and fear. Our ability to allow ourselves to feel good and to have things consistently is grossly underdeveloped. Case in point, read through the following statements. As you do, take notice of how true or false the following statements feel to you:

I can feel God's presence all of the time.

I can feel good mentally, emotionally, and physically all of the time.

Things can go well in my life all of the time.

In relationships, I can live in harmony and intimacy all of the time.

I can live in expanding waves of peace and prosperity, free from fear and dread.

If you are like most people, one or more of these statements will reveal to you there's a roadblock that keeps you from expecting God's best all the time. You, over time, have developed a subconscious belief that things will eventually go bad. Unknowingly, you rely on this belief as a protection mechanism that helps you avoid unnecessary disappointment and pain. Without realizing it, you have a subconscious habit of expecting the worst so that you are prepared for the bad news that you expect will inevitably come your way.

While this might be an effective way of self-protection, it also poses a big problem. It limits our ability to believe in God's goodness and receive increasingly good things in our lives. It also drastically limits what we believe God can do through our lives. If we are going to make the journey, reach our full potential in Christ, and possess the Promised Land God has for us, it's super-important that we confront and break through this roadblock.

How the Roadblock Was Installed

Because so few people are aware of this roadblock, most people believe they are flawed, not destined for greatness, or simply not good enough to deserve the dreams God has placed in their hearts. Others miss out on big-time success and chalk it up to bad luck or bad timing. Millions of people are stuck on the verge of reaching their dreams, yet fall short because they are struggling under an invisible glass ceiling – the roadblock that has yet to be revealed. But here's the good news – you're not flawed or unlucky or anything of the sort. You are in Christ! Your potential is unlimited. You can break through the roadblock in the wink of an eye. All the Holy Spirit needs is an open and willing heart.

So how does this roadblock get installed in the first place? That's an interesting question worth considering. All of us, whether we are aware of it or not, have an inner thermostat setting that determines how much love, success, and creativity we allow ourselves to enjoy. When we exceed our inner thermostat setting, we will often do something to sabotage ourselves, causing us to drop back into the old, familiar zone where we feel secure. This internal thermostat setting was programmed in early childhood, before we could really think for ourselves. Once programmed, this thermostat setting holds us back from enjoying all the love, financial abundance, and creativity that's rightfully ours in Christ. It prevents us from living the unbelievably good life that the Father planned for us.

What you need to recognize is this: If you make miraculous progress in one area of your life, your internal thermostat will quickly kick in. Unless the roadblock is dealt with, it will keep you from enjoying your new level of abundance. Feelings of self-doubt, unworthiness, and guilt will steal it from you. Guilt oftentimes operates in conjunction with a roadblock. When we're feeling good for making extra money or feeling a deeper loving connection in a relationship, for example, we'll suddenly hit the hidden barrier of an old belief such as, "I must not feel good, because fundamentally flawed people like me don't deserve it."

When the old belief clashes with the positive feelings you're enjoying, one of them has to win. If the old belief wins, you end up doing something to sabotage your progress. You might lose some money or start an intimacy-destroying argument with your partner. But if you recognize the old belief for what it is and make the decision to enjoy your progress, congratulations! You just broke through the roadblock!

Most people think they will finally feel good when they have more money, better relationships, and more creativity. What a powerful moment it is, though, when we finally see that we have it the wrong way around. With the Holy Spirit's help, we can develop the capacity to feel good and enjoy life right now. We don't have to wait until some longed-for event occurs. God's goodness can be experienced anytime. The Father longs for us to experience wave after wave of greater love, creative energy, and financial abundance, without the compulsion to sabotage ourselves.

Going Deeper

As we wrap up this chapter, I'd like you to take a moment to reflect on how important it is to recognize and overcome the detours, breakdowns, and roadblocks as you pursue your divine destiny. Everyone struggles to believe the outrageous almost too-good-to-be-true plan God has for their life. What's important is to tune in to your inner world and develop self-awareness. Partner with the Holy Spirit and allow Him to expose the self-limiting beliefs you believe about yourself, God, and His purpose and plan for your life. As you do, there is absolutely nothing that can hold you back from enjoying the fullness of who you are in Christ and living the life of your dreams.

Love Letter from God

My Blessed Child,

The path I'm leading you down to reach your destiny is called The Path of Wholeness. As you follow me step by step down this path, I will help you overcome the breakdowns, detours, and roadblocks you encounter along the way. And, while this path may not be the shortest route, you will be so happy that you chose to follow Me. Success with freedom feels so much better than success without it. Wholeness feels incredible and is worth taking the time to pursue. What's the hurry anyway? I promise you'll reach your destiny just at the right time if you'll continue to follow Me.

My purpose and vision for your life is going to make your brain go "tilt" on many occasions. That is the thing about the impossible. Even trying to wrap your mind around it seems impossible sometimes. So, why in the world would I call you to do something that's impossible for you to do? Because, beloved, I want you to believe in something bigger than you. I want you to believe in Me. I want you to believe that I am exactly who I claim to be – a good, good Father, who has your best interests in mind.

When Moses asked to see My glory, I told Him I would make all My goodness pass before Him. That's because My glory is My goodness. My glory isn't intangible, it's experienceable. When you experience My goodness, I am glorified. My desire for you goes way beyond you living the life of your dreams. I want you to experience ALL that Jesus died for you to experience – perfect wholeness, perfect peace, and perfect love. Anything less than heaven on earth falls short of what's in My heart for you.

Kisses from Heaven,
Dad

Digging Deeper Exercise 1 – Overcoming the Grasshopper Syndrome

In this exercise, we are going to ask ourselves four very simple but powerful questions that will help identity the grasshopper syndrome in your own life. As you reflect on your answers with the Holy Spirit, give Him permission to reveal and transform the underlying self-limiting beliefs that are hindering you from reaching your destiny and experiencing God's best.

STEP 1 – Set the Atmosphere
Find a quiet place where you can be alone and focus.

- Set aside a few moments to get yourself in the right frame of mind.
- The goal is to clear your mind of distractions and connect with your spirit.
- Consider having soft, worshipful music playing in the background or lighting a candle.
- Once you feel connected and can sense God's presence, focus on His presence.
- Allow His presence to saturate your entire being.
- Become aware of union with Jesus.
- Hide in Him, then see Him in you.
- Allow yourself to be enveloped in His love.
- Stay in this place as long as needed. His presence is life.

When you sense the Holy Spirit's leading, move to the next step.

STEP 2 – Open in Prayer
From a place of union with Jesus, pray the following prayer out loud. As you pray, stay aware of what the Holy Spirit shows you. If you receive inspired imaginations, make sure to write or draw what you see in your journal.

Holy Spirit, Today, I am here abiding in Jesus, believing and trusting in the Father's extravagant goodness. However, I have experienced many things that have taught me to expect less than heaven on earth. As a result, I've experienced life as a roller coaster where the good is often followed by something bad. I've learned to settle for less than Jesus' abundant life. However, today I am expecting You to set me free and help me experience new levels of freedom. Lead and guide me into all truth. Help my unbelief. Open my eyes to the reality of the Father's goodness. Show me a future that goes from glory to glory and faith to faith. Make it so it's the exception for me to feel bad and normal for me to feel joyful, peaceful, and content. Delete the programs that have held me captive. Install new ones that make experiencing abundant life normal for me. In Jesus' name, AMEN!

STEP 3 - Expose Lies

Start with a new page in your journal with today's date on it. Ask the Holy Spirit to help you fill in the blank for the following statement.

I cannot expand to my full potential in Christ and fulfill my destiny because _____.

As you fill in the blank, recognize the phrase you speak may trigger the feelings attached to this belief. You will most likely find that just by saying the belief out loud, you will have stirred up some negative, sad, or humiliating feelings and possibly a few memories. If this happens, don't panic. You didn't do anything wrong. It simply means you just hit the nail on the head and identified a self-limiting belief.

Write down your completed phrase in your journal.

STEP 4 - Hear from the Holy Spirit

Once you have filled in the above phrase, ask the Holy Spirit the following questions and write down whatever He shows you:

- Why do I believe this statement?
- Where did I learn this about myself? Is there a specific memory you want to show me?
- Who do I need to forgive as a result of what happened?
- Take some time to forgive whoever needs to be forgiven, including God and yourself if appropriate, praying the following prayer:

Holy Spirit, I choose by an act of my will to forgive (insert names) for (insert what you need to forgive) and for teaching me (insert the negative things you learned about yourself). I release all of this to You, along with the (insert painful emotions and consequences) that were caused as a result. Take back the ground that was stolen as a result of what happened. Establish Your kingdom in this area of my heart and life. In Jesus' name, AMEN!

- If the Holy Spirit showed you a specific memory, ask Jesus to now show up in the memory. What is He doing?
- What is the truth that you want to tell me about the lie I believe?
- Ask the Holy Spirit to show you the way you really are – completely free of whatever the area of bondage, unbelief, or wrong thinking might be
- Write down whatever the Holy Spirit shows you.

Digging Deeper Exercise 2 – Schedule a Rethink RMR Session (Optional)

In this next exercise, which is optional, you are invited to schedule a Rethink RMR session to help you walk in greater levels of wholeness and freedom. Although this step is optional, it is highly recommended. As I stated earlier, a Rethink RMR session is a powerful way to partner with the Holy Spirit to identity and overcome breakdowns, detours, and roadblocks. To schedule your session, email us at transformation@schlyce.com or call (719) 286-0084.

CHAPTER TEN

Embracing the Adventure

The big question is whether you are going to be able to say
a hearty yes to your adventure.
– Joseph Campbell

Walking with God down the path that leads to the fulfillment of your divine destiny is one of life's greatest adventures. Sure, there are twists, turns, obstacles, and all kinds of surprises that you will encounter on the journey. But, this is what makes your life story an action adventure. Your life is meant to be intriguing, exciting, and inspiring. Living a mundane, safe, little life is b-o-r-i-n-g. True fulfillment isn't found in playing it safe. It's living a life without regrets.

Don't ever, ever forget, the Greater One lives in you. This means you were born for greatness. The Jesus *in you* has already overcome every single obstacle you will face on the way to your destiny. Absolutely nothing can stop you from living the life of your dreams, except you. So, go for it! Live fearlessly and pursue your dreams with all your heart. Become everything that God created you to be. Live a life that reveals the glory of God within you and inspires others to do the same.

Be Yourself

Never, and I mean never, compare yourself to other people. It's completely ridiculous! Can I say it again? It is ridiculous for you to compare yourself or compete with anyone. You are not in competition with anyone to become you! Your life purpose is about you becoming *you* and releasing *your* full potential. What does that have to do with anyone else? You are not in a race against anyone to release your full potential. There is only one of you. No one else can be you, so comparing yourself to others makes absolutely no sense whatsoever. You emerging into the fullness of who God created you to be *is the only goal*.

Whatever path you have to travel down and whatever lessons you have to learn and whatever obstacles you have to overcome are perfect. It's all a part of you discovering how glorious you are. So be kind to yourself and do yourself a favor. Don't play the comparison game.

> *Don't compare yourself with others. Just look at your own work to see if you have done anything to be proud of. You must each accept the responsibilities that are yours.*
> – Galatians 6:4–5 (ERV)

What's Next, Papa?

I love the following scripture. I have it written on sticky notes that are stuck to my mirror and my office desk. The reason I love it so much is because it reminds me to slow down, breathe, and stay connected to the Father's heart.

> *The resurrection life you received from God is not a timid, grave-tending life. It's adventurously expectant, greeting God with a childlike, "What's next, Papa?" God's Spirit touches our spirits and confirms who we really are. We know who He is, and we know who we are: Father and children. And we know we are going to get what's coming to us — an unbelievable inheritance! We go through exactly what Christ goes through. If we go through the hard times with him, then we're certainly going to go through the good times with him!*
> – Romans 8:15–18 (MSG)

I think the Message Translation of this scripture is the best, especially the phrase "What's next, Papa?" It keeps me from getting overwhelmed or confused and keeps me dependent on the Father and His instructions. It helps me stay on track and not get ahead of God. It is a comforting reminder – all that we need to do to reach our destiny is follow God's step-by-step instructions.

It's true. Staying awake to God's presence and following His lead is really all we need to remember. The thing about life being an adventure is this: Adventures, like life, are unpredictable. There are always things that are going to come up and that's okay as long as we remember Who is with us. Romans 8:15–18 encourages us to fearlessly embrace and treat every day like the exciting adventure it is.

When you wake up every morning, expect God's best. Say, "Good morning, Papa! What do you have up your sleeve for today?" Then hop out of bed and face the day, expecting God to show up in amazing ways. When you face opposition, don't get discouraged. Instead look at it as an opportunity for God to be God. Don't allow anything to separate you from God's love or stop your forward progress. You are God's masterpiece. Your life is a work in progress that is getting more glorious day by day. Don't despise today's glory. Embrace it! Embrace the journey and expect God's best.

Don't Give Up

Lastly, the most important advice I can leave you with as we end this leg of our journey together is this: Make a decision right now, before you finish this book, that you will never ever quit pursuing your life purpose. No matter how many times you get knocked down, you will get up and by the grace of God keep going. I love what Heidi Baker says. She says, "If you don't quit, you win!" I totally agree. Half the battle is to just keep on going. Ignore the critics, tune out the naysayers, and don't listen to the voice of the accuser. Trust God, apply the things God has shown you, and keep fighting the good fight of faith.

Each and every encounter you've had with God as you read this book was purposeful, strategic, and significant. You experienced the things you experienced for specific reasons. I encourage you, now that you've finished the book, to take some time to go back and review, reflect, and digest the things God revealed to you. Any time you encounter God or have a conversation with Him, you can always go back and glean more. It is like sitting down with any other friend or loved one – you can pick up the conversation where you left off and learn more about the other person or the topic you were discussing. Remember the old saying, "Hindsight is 20/20?" When it comes to pursuing the path of purpose, this is definitely true. The things God has revealed to you will become more clear as you walk out your destiny.

The path of the righteous is like the morning sun,
shining ever brighter till the full light of day.
– Proverbs 4:18 (NIV)

This scripture highlights this point. As you pursue your destiny, step by step, things will become clearer and clearer. Over time, you will gain a deeper understanding and appreciation of the things God has shown you. You can also expect the Holy Spirit to remind you of these things and expound on them as time progresses.

This is why it's so very important, and I can't encourage you enough, to continue the habit of spending quality time with God. Make your intimacy with God your top priority and make sure you are experiencing your union with Jesus, Papa, and the Holy Spirit on a daily basis. There's always more of God to know and experience. And staying awake to God's presence, the realm of the Spirit, and your true identity in Christ is a daily exercise.

It's your time to shine, beloved, so get excited about the things God has in store for you. Expect to experience God's goodness in unbelievable ways and for Him to bless a whole lot of people as the Jesus in you is released through you. You can be all that God created you to be. You can do all that God's created you to do. You were God's idea and He will finish the good work He began in you and bring it to completion. Faithful is He who called you; He will also do it.

And I am certain that God, who began the good work within you, will continue his
work until it is finally finished on the day when Christ Jesus returns.
– Philippians 1:6 (NLT)

He who calls you is faithful; he will surely do it.
– 1 Thessalonians 5:24 (ESV)

Love Letter from God

My Favored Child,

There is nothing holding you back from heading down the path that leads to your destiny and living the life I created you to live. So come on, child, let's go! Buckle up, child, and get ready to go on the adventure of a lifetime. You don't have to bring a thing. I'll be providing everything you need. I prearranged it, actually, so we are all set.

You are about to experience a level of acceleration in your life that may make your head spin. It may even seem like things are moving too fast. But don't be alarmed. There are no speed limits or red lights on your path for a reason. You are living under my divine "Yes!" You have My permission to pursue your dreams. It's just green light, after green light, after green light.

I know you want to know the way to where I am taking you, but that would steal the surprise. Knowing the destination is all that matters. That way, you can just relax and enjoy the ride. Being together and enjoying each other's company is what makes the journey memorable. Trust me, we'll get there just at the right time, even if it seems like it took a while.

Before we get started, there's something very important I want you to remember. I am so pleased with you. I am so proud to be your Dad. I love that we are taking this journey together. I love spending time with you. I love revealing My heart to you. I love sharing your life with you. But most of all, I just love you. With everything I AM, I love you

Kisses from Heaven,
Dad

Digging Deeper Exercise – Your Answers to the 5 Big Qs

In this last Digging Deeper Exercise, you are going to write your own God-breathed answers to each of the 5 Big Qs. As you contemplate how you will answer each of the 5 Big Qs, keep in mind, the goal is to articulate your answer clearly and concisely, in just a couple of sentences.

STEP 1 – Set the Atmosphere

Before beginning, you will want to set the atmosphere:

- Set aside a few moments to get yourself in the right frame of mind.
- The goal is to clear your mind of distractions and connect with your spirit.
- Consider having soft, worshipful music playing in the background or lighting a candle.

Once you feel connected and can sense God's presence, you're ready to move to the next step.

STEP 2 – Pray

Pray the following prayer out loud.

Holy Spirit, As I endeavor to develop my answer to each of the 5 Big Qs today, guide the process. Lead me into all truth. Think through my mind and help me articulate Your thoughts in writing. Enlighten my eyes so that I can see things from Your perspective. Show me the work you've done in me and empower me to clearly communicate my answers to the 5 Big Qs. In Jesus' name, AMEN!

STEP 3 – Review Your Work

Write down each one of the 5 Big Qs at the top of a new page in your journal.

1st Big Q – Who is God?
2nd Big Q – Who am I?
3rd Big Q – Why am I here?

4th Big Q – Where am I headed?
5th Big Q – How do I get there?

Next, take some time to review the work you completed in each of the Qs. As you review your work, jot down key ideas and concepts that the Holy Spirit highlights to you in your journal. Afterward, begin to craft your answer to each of the 5 Big Qs, keeping in mind the goal is to clearly and concisely articulate your answer to each of the Qs in less than two minutes.

STEP 4 – Write Down Your Answers

Write down the answer you crafted to each of the 5 Big Qs in your journal. When you are finished, pat yourself on the back. Congratulations are in order. You discovered your very own God-breathed answers to The 5 Big Qs of Life!

TRANSLATION INDEX

Throughout *The Path*, the author references multiple Bible translations to help accurately convey the depth of meaning of various scriptures. Here is an explanation of abbreviations for the translations used:

AMP – The Amplified Bible

CEB – The Common English Bible

ESV – English Standard Version

KJV – King James Version

MSG – The Message Translation

NASB – New American Standard Bible

NIV – New International Version

NKJV – New King James Version

NLT – New Living Translation

NLV – New Life Version

TPT – The Passion Translation

TEB – The Transparent English Bible

Voice – The Voice

WEB – Word English Bible

ACKNOWLEDGMENTS

This book would not have been possible without the tireless support of the Emerge launch team and their passionate belief in our common cause to represent Jesus as love and the gospel as good news. Catherine Toon, Mercy McKee, Amy Tompkins, Kris Turner, Tracey Irvin, Rachel Enlow, Heath Enlow, Jason Hensley, Yeahmah Logan, and Sandy Myers – Emerge would have never gotten off the ground or been the basis of this book without all of your beautiful sacrifices. The words *thank you* fall hopelessly short in conveying just how much your never-ending belief in me and the vision of Emerge has meant to me. I love and appreciate each of you so much.

To all of the Emergers who have graduated or are currently enrolled, thank you for trusting me with the most intimate and sacred details of your life. Seeing you face and overcome your greatest fears and allow Jesus to transform your hearts and minds is the biggest privilege of my life. Your stories inspired every page of this book.

I would also like to thank my spiritual fathers, mothers, and mentors – Dr. Bill Winston, Pastor Joe Barlow, Paul Milligan, Bishop Jamie Englehart, Nathan Blouse, Susan King, and Mark and Nancy Campbell – for the part you played in helping me discover my own God-breathed answers to the 5 Big Qs of Life. You gave me permission to follow my heart, not fit in, and blaze a new trail. Words cannot express my gratitude to all of you for all of the things you have taught me over the years. I have experienced the Father's heart through each of you in so many tangible ways.

To the Morgan James Publishing team: Special thanks to David Hancock, CEO & Founder for believing in me and my message. To my Author Relations Manager, Tiffany Gibson, thanks for making the process seamless and easy. Many more thanks to everyone else, but especially Jim Howard, Bethany Marshall, and Nickcole Watkins.

Another person who greatly influenced this book, who probably has no idea just how much she has taught me over the years, is my sister-in-love, Reagan. Thank you for second, third, fourth, and fifth chances. It's truly a miracle that our relationship survived the religious roller-coaster ride I was on for more than a decade. It wasn't pretty and I will never forget what being a Pharisee felt like or the impact that it had on the best friend I had ever had. I am committed to spending the rest of our years together having fun, being family, and making up for lost time.

Above all, I am thankful for my beautiful family – my dad, Roy, my husband, Brian, and our two amazing girls – Lily Simone and Ella Skye. Your unconditional love has healed my heart. Thank you for being my biggest fans and for saying yes to God's dream for our family. You are my joy and delight – the spice and sizzle of my life. Our journey together is always an adventure. You are God's best gifts to me.

ABOUT THE AUTHOR

Schlyce Jimenez is a rebel with a cause – to reveal what the Father is really like. As a speaker, author, and transformation coach, Schlyce empowers big dreamers to make a difference in the world the same way Jesus did – through oneness with the Father. Over the years, she has helped thousands of people experience God for themselves. Schlyce's greatest passion is seeing the full potential of Christ revealed in people's lives, especially those who haven't met Him yet or who think He's someone He's not.

Her groundbreaking work, as founder of Emerge School of Transformation and CEO of Rethink, is unlocking the inner genius, creativity, and full potential of tomorrow's masterminds, change agents, and cultural movers and shakers. Her relentless pursuit to destroy the spirit of religion and correct the way it wrongly portrays God's heart has at times cast Schlyce in the role of renegade and rebel. But like Jesus, Schlyce is unleashing world changers who are divinely destined to leave an indelible mark on humanity. Her clients include CEOs, inventors, authors, pastors, entrepreneurs, artists, photographers, musicians, counselors, movie actors and directors, and multimillionaires, just to name a few.

Schlyce's life vision is simple and impossible just the way God planned it – "To make planet earth look like heaven and cause love to rule the world."

She and her husband, Brian, when they are not going 90-to-nothing changing the world one life at a time, delight in parenting their two beautiful girls, Lily Simone and Ella Skye. As a family, they enjoy spending time together, going to movies, and taking in the beauty of Colorado on hikes, on mountain bikes, or on skis/snowboards. Schlyce loves a good vanilla latte and dressing Queen Kaydie, her 4-pound yorkie poo, in the fanciest and most ridiculous outfits she can find.

ABOUT EMERGE SCHOOL OF TRANSFORMATION

Emerge School of Transformation empowers spiritual seekers from all walks of life to discover their life purpose through a deeper "religion-free" relationship with God. Emerge's Spirit-centered approach to self-actualization was developed from the ground up by Schlyce Jimenez. For over 25 years as a transformational business coach, Schlyce has been helping today's leaders and future world changers fulfill their life missions and take their organizations to the next level.

Different by design, Emerge's curriculum will to lead you step by glorious step into finding your own God-breathed answers to the "The 5 Big Qs of Life" through personal encounters with God. In the process, you will develop the same kind of intimate relationship that Jesus enjoyed with the Father so that you, like Jesus, can discover and live your life purpose to make a difference in the world. The Emerge experience will lead you into the adventure of a lifetime, where you live the one and only life you've been given to the fullest and release the full potential of Christ in you.

To find out more about Emerge and apply to be a part of this life-changing program, go to https://www.schlyce.com/apply.

ABOUT RETHINK
RAPID MIND RENEWAL (RMR) SESSIONS

A Rethink RMR session is a two-hour facilitated encounter with God that helps you uncover memories and negative beliefs, both conscious and subconscious, that are driving negative behaviors, causing you pain, or limiting you in some way. Once these areas are uncovered, our certified facilitators use the tools within the Rapid Mind Renewal Framework to bring you to a new place of peace, wholeness, and freedom.

The RMR Framework is a groundbreaking Spirit-centered approach to supernatural mind renewal that incorporates the way God created our minds to work and be renewed. Recognizing the validity of neuroplasticity and modern neuroscience, which explains how mind renewal works, the RMR Framework releases the transformation described in Romans 12:2 instantaneously, through the power of God. The RMR Framework is based on the pioneering ministry and methodologies developed by Nathan Blouse, founder of The Safe Place (www.inthesafeplace.com).

To find out more or schedule a Rethink RMR session, email us at transformation@schlyce.com. Sessions are offered in person, online, and over the phone.

THANK YOU

My Gift to You for Reading *The Path*

I'd love to hear your answers to the 5 Big Qs, see your Life Vision Board, and learn more about the dream life God designed for you to live. To get my personal feedback, please email me at info@schlyce.com or comment on my Facebook page at https://www.facebook.com/Schlyce.

FREE VIDEO CLASS To sign up for the FREE companion video training for The Path, head over: to: https://www.schlyce.com/thepathvideo

Printed in the USA
CPSIA information can be obtained
at www.ICGtesting.com
JSHW082229140824
68134JS00017B/808